Benevolent Benefactor
or Insensitive Regulator?
Tracing the Role of Government
Policies in the Development
of India's Automobile Industry

About the East-West Center
The East-West Center promotes better relations and understanding among the people and nations of the United States, Asia, and the Pacific through cooperative study, research, and dialogue. Established by the U.S. Congress in 1960, the Center serves as a resource for information and analysis on critical issues of common concern, bringing people together to exchange views, build expertise, and develop policy options.

The Center's 21-acre Honolulu campus, adjacent to the University of Hawai'i at Mānoa, is located midway between Asia and the U.S. mainland and features research, residential, and international conference facilities. The Center's Washington, D.C., office focuses on preparing the United States for an era of growing Asia Pacific prominence.

The Center is an independent, public, nonprofit organization with funding from the U.S. government, and additional support provided by private agencies, individuals, foundations, corporations, and governments in the region.

Policy Studies 58

Benevolent Benefactor or Insensitive Regulator?
Tracing the Role of Government Policies in the Development of India's Automobile Industry

Rajnish Tiwari, Cornelius Herstatt,
and Mahipat Ranawat

Benevolent Benefactor or Insensitive Regulator?
Tracing the Role of Government Policies
in the Development of India's Automobile Industry
by Rajnish Tiwari, Cornelius Herstatt, and Mahipat Ranawat

ISSN 1547-1349 (print) and 1547-1330 (electronic)
ISBN 978-1-932728-90-3 (print) and 978-1-932728-91-0 (electronic)

East-West Center
1601 East-West Road
Honolulu, Hawai'i 96848-1601
Tel: 808.944.7111
EWCInfo@EastWestCenter.org
EastWestCenter.org/policystudies

The views expressed are those of the author(s) and not necessarily those of the Center.

Hard copies of publications in the series are available through Amazon.com.

In Asia, hard copies of all titles, and electronic copies of select Southeast Asia titles, co-published in Singapore, are available through:

Institute of Southeast Asian Studies
30 Heng Mui Keng Terrace
Pasir Panjang Road, Singapore 119614
Email: publish@iseas.edu.sg
Website: http://bookshop.iseas.edu.sg

Contents

List of Acronyms

ACMA	Automotive Component Manufacturers Association of India
ARAI	Automotive Research Association of India
ATMA	Automotive Tyre Manufacturers' Association (of India)
CAGR	compounded annual growth rate
CBUs	completely built units
CKD	completely knocked-down (kits)
CVs	commercial vehicles
FDI	foreign direct investment
FERA	Foreign Exchange Regulation Act
FYP	Five-Year Plan
GOI	Government of India
HCVs	heavy commercial vehicles
HML	Hindustan Motors Ltd.
IBEF	India Brand Equity Foundation
IDRA	Industries (Development and Regulation) Act of 1951

IMF	International Monetary Fund
INR	Indian national rupees
IPR	Industrial Policy Resolution
LCVs	light commercial vehicles
M&M	Mahindra and Mahindra
MCVs	medium commercial vehicles
MICO	Motor Industries Company Ltd.
MoU	memorandum of understanding
MRTP	Monopolies and Restrictive Trade Practices Act
MUL	Maruti Udyog Ltd.
NATRiP	National Automotive Testing and R&D Infrastructure Development Project
OECD	Organisation for Economic Co-Operation and Development
OEMs	original equipment manufacturers
OGL	open general license
OICA	Organisation Internationale des Constructeurs d'Automobiles (International Organization of Motor Vehicle Manufacturers)
PAL	Premier Automobiles Ltd.
PVs	passenger vehicles
R&D	research and development
RBI	Reserve Bank of India
SIAM	Society of Indian Automobile Manufacturers
SKD	semi knocked-down (kits)

TELCO	Tata Engineering and Locomotive Company
UVs	utility vehicles
WTO	World Trade Organization

Executive Summary

India's automobile industry has witnessed an impressive run of sustained growth in the past two decades. The total number of vehicles produced in fiscal year 1990–91 was only 2.3 million, but by fiscal year 2009–10 this number had swelled to 14.1 million. Similarly, the value of automotive products exported by India was only US$198 million in 1990, but by 2009 the value had increased nearly twenty-five-fold to US$5 billion, representing an average annual growth rate of 26 percent and catapulting India into the league of the top fifteen exporters of automotive products worldwide.

The turning point in the fortunes of India's automotive sector was arguably the policy of economic liberalization initiated in 1991. The reforms were introduced in the wake of a severe financial crisis, which forced India to gradually dismantle its protectionist regime, do away with the "license raj," and to actively seek foreign direct investment (FDI). It is generally acknowledged in the literature that this liberalization process had a significantly positive impact on the automobile sector. This impact might not have been possible, however, if India had not nurtured its automobile industry in the first place and if it had not ensured that a more or less competitive industry basis existed in the country when the automobile sector was fully liberalized by 2002. In this respect, India's policy steps since independence in 1947 are in many ways comparable to those of other, developing countries in Latin America and Southeast Asia—albeit with some differing results. For instance, even though India started relatively late with its economic reforms, the Indian automobile industry quickly came to terms with globalization.

The present study seeks to identify the changes in India's policy regimes in the postindependence era to understand their impact on India's automobile industry. Using a policy framework based on Michael E. Porter's "Diamond" model of national competitiveness, this study identifies various supporting (and in some instances inhibiting) regulatory conditions imposed by the Indian government in various phases of the industry's evolution. Where feasible, these steps are compared with actions taken by governments in other developing and emerging countries and by some developed countries like Japan in the formation period of the automobile industry, so as to illustrate the similarities and differences in the development paths.

The study concludes that in India the government has played a key role in the evolution of the automobile industry. In the postindependence era, it was in an overregulation mode, sometimes motivated by ideological reasons and at other times constrained by fiscal resources, stifling domestic competition, shutting the door on foreign firms, and even regulating price. With the benefit of hindsight, it might be argued that the protectionist policies followed by successive governments in the prereform era did cause considerable opportunity costs for the Indian automobile industry, for the consumers, and for the state itself.

On the other hand, especially in comparison with some other developing nations that gained independence from colonial rule at about the same time, the government has been relatively successful in creating and sustaining favorable innovation systems at national, regional, and sectoral levels. With its insistence on indigenization in the prereform era, it managed to sustain a significant domestic base that has been able to withstand the competitive pressure in the postliberalization period and has also even managed to expand overseas. The foreign automobile sector firms that have invested in India have been able to operate without many strings attached and have significantly contributed to the upgrading of the sectoral innovation system. The government has played a proactive role in supporting outward FDI by Indian automotive firms. Of late, there has been considerable support in government circles for product innovation and formal research and development activities. In particular, the segment of compact small cars has seen fiscal incentives, such as a reduced rate of excise duties, and the government would like to see India emerge as an innovation and production hub for small cars. Moreover, investments in the basic infrastructure, such as roads and highways, have also provided a boost to the automobile industry.

Two interesting aspects about the government's impact on the development of the automobile industry in India make it appear to be a "benevolent benefactor" at certain times and may be summarized as follows.

1. The Indian government, unlike its counterparts in many other developing nations, has not concentrated its attempts singularly on influencing the industry structures or creating local supplier industries. Its policy measures especially since the 1990s, and to a greater extent than those of some other developing nations, have tried to actively create favorable factor and demand conditions, thereby strengthening the local market and giving a key impetus to the development of the industry.

2. India put an early focus on some specific segments of the automobile industry. This focus, in a protected environment, gave rise to strong domestic players, who were able to take advantage of the liberalization gradually injected at a later stage. The specialization effects seem to be helping India's industry succeed globally, especially in the two-wheeler and small car segments.

Nonetheless, the government would be well advised to continue and even intensify the reform process. An enhanced thrust on innovations is required more than ever, in order to upgrade the safety and emission norms while allowing for products affordable for larger sections of the society within the country. Raising safety and environmental standards could help reduce negative country-of-origin effects sometimes associated with products made in India and provide better access to other global markets, which could potentially see India emerge as a "lead market" for compact small cars.

Benevolent Benefactor or Insensitive Regulator?
Tracing the Role of Government Policies in the Development of India's Automobile Industry

Introduction

India's automobile industry has witnessed an impressive run of sustained growth in the previous two decades. While the total number of vehicles produced in fiscal year 1990–91 was 2.3 million, including two-and three-wheelers (cf., Ranawat and Tiwari 2009: 54), this number had swelled to 14.1 million units by fiscal 2009–10 (SIAM 2010b).[1] Similarly, while India exported US$198 million worth of automotive products in 1990 (WTO 2001: 141), the export value had increased nearly twenty-five-fold to US$5 billion by 2009, catapulting India into the league of the top fifteen exporters of automotive products worldwide (WTO 2010: 101). According to the same report of the World Trade Organization (WTO 2010), India's automotive exports grew on average 26 percent a year between 2000 and 2009.

The turning point in the fortunes of India's automotive sector was arguably the policy of economic liberalization initiated in 1991 (see, e.g., D'Costa 1995; Narayanan 1998; Sutton 2005). The reforms were introduced in the wake of a severe financial crisis, which forced India to gradually dismantle its protectionist regime, to do away with the "license raj," and to actively seek foreign direct investment (FDI) (Ahluwalia 2002, 2006). It is generally acknowledged in the literature that this liberalization process has had a significantly positive impact on the automobile sector (see, e.g., Narayanan 2004; Rasiah and Kumar 2008).

However, this impact might not have been possible had India not nurtured its automobile industry in the first place and had it not ensured that a more or less competitive industry basis existed in the country when the automobile sector was fully liberalized by 2002. In this respect, India's policy steps since independence in 1947 are in many ways comparable to those of other developing countries in Latin America and Southeast Asia—however, with some differing results. For instance, even though India started relatively late with its economic reforms, the Indian automobile industry has been quick to come to terms with globalization. Its 2.6 million units

India started relatively late with economic reforms, but its automobile industry quickly came to terms with globalization

made it the seventh largest producer of four-wheelers worldwide in 2009, advancing from fifteenth position in 1999 (OICA 2000, 2010a). Among the group of developing, and newly industrialized economies, only South Korea (3.5 million units) and Brazil (3.2 million units) produced more four-wheelers in 2009 than India.

The discussion above gives us reason to believe that at least some part of this success story can be attributed to policy factors. The important role government policies (or the absence thereof) play in shaping the development of a nation's industries is well established in the academic literature (see for instance Doz and Prahalad 1980, Doz 1986, Porter 1990, Nelson 1993, Rodrik 1995, Lall 2003, and Rasiah and Amin 2010). To put it in the words of Yves Doz (1986: 226): "Government intervention … creates both constraints and opportunities, and also modifies the relative attractiveness of various options. Governments also have a sufficient impact on the evolution of industry structures, and on the nature of rivalry within industries to make a careful consideration of their actions—current and potential—of critical importance."

Extending this line of thought also to previous policies, this paper seeks to identify the relevant changes in policy regimes in the postindependence era in order to understand their impact on India's automobile industry. Using a policy framework based on Porter (1990), this paper identifies the various supporting, and in some instances inhibiting, regulatory conditions imposed by the Indian government in various phases of industry evolution since 1947. Where feasible, these steps are compared with actions taken by governments in other developing and emerging countries (Doner 1988, 1991; Jenkins 1977, 1987; Rasiah 2007, 2009; Rasiah and Amin 2010) and by some developed countries like Japan in the formation period of the automobile industry (Odagiri and Goto 1993) so as to illustrate the similarities and differences in the development paths. The objective is to understand the role that policy factors have played and continue to play in the development of this increasingly important industry.

This study comes to the conclusion that in India the government has played a key role in the evolution of the automobile industry. In the postindependence era, the government was in an overregulation mode—at least to some extent, sometimes motivated by ideological reasons and at other times constrained by fiscal resources—stifling domestic competition, shutting the doors on foreign firms, and even regulating prices. With the benefit of hindsight, it might be argued that protectionist policies followed by the successive governments in the prereform era caused considerable opportunity costs for the Indian automobile industry, for the consumers, and for the state itself.

On the other hand, especially in comparison with many other developing nations that gained independence from colonial rule at about the same time, the government has been relatively successful in creating or supporting favorable innovation systems, or doing both, at national, regional, and sectoral levels. With its insistence on indigenization in the prereform era, it has managed to sustain a significant domestic base, which has been able to withstand the competitive pressure in the postliberalization period and has also even managed to expand overseas. The foreign automobile sector firms that have invested in India have been largely able to operate without many strings attached and have significantly contributed to the upgrading of the sectoral innovation system. The government has played a proactive role in supporting outward FDI by Indian automotive firms. Of late, there has been considerable support in government circles for product innovations and formal research and development (R&D). In particular, the segment of compact small cars has seen fiscal incentives, such as a reduced rate of excise duties, and the government would like to see India emerge as an innovation and production hub for compact cars. Moreover, investments in basic infrastructure, such as roads and highways, have also provided a boost to the automobile industry.

The government's policies for promoting certain segments of the automobile industry (e.g., two-wheelers and later small cars) in a protected environment have ensured the emergence of strong domestic players who are now globally competitive. Second, the government has actively worked on the creation of better factor conditions and has, since the 1980s, tried to stimulate demand. The ensuing effects point in the direction of a benevolent benefactor, even though at times they may have been merely unintended side-effects of policies initiated in a different context.

Nonetheless, the government would be well advised to continue the reform process. An enhanced thrust on innovations is required more than ever in order to upgrade the security and emission norms while allowing for products affordable for larger sections of the society within the country. While private sector firms, both domestic and foreign-owned, are actively pursuing development and design activities in India, they are often faced with a shortage of skilled and experienced engineers. The government would be well advised to intensify efforts to upgrade India's base of skilled labor, including the blue-collar segment. Raising safety and environmental standards could help reduce negative country-of-origin effects sometimes associated with products made in India and provide better access to other global markets that could potentially see India emerge as a "lead market" for compact small cars.

The rest of the paper is organized in the following manner. The second section provides an overview of the relevant policy factors, which serve as a framework for the subsequent analysis. The third section gives a snapshot of the developments in the Indian automobile industry. The fourth section deals with government policies related to the automotive industry in various phases. The paper concludes with a summarizing analysis in the fifth section.

Role of Policy Factors in Industry Development

The important role government policies[2] (or the absence thereof) play in shaping the development of a nation's industries is well established in the academic literature (cf., Doz 1986; Doz and Prahalad 1980; Evans 1995; Gilpin 1971; Lall 2003; Nelson 1993; Porter 1990; Rasiah n.d.; Rasiah and Amin 2010; Rodrik 1995).[3] This role is very well characterized in the words of Robert Gilpin (1996: 416), who has given an interesting description of the American economic model:

> The American model of the economy rests on the assumption that competitive markets exist and, if not, should be made to exist. Any economic activity is permitted unless it is specifically forbidden. With respect to the outside world, the economy is assumed to be open unless specifically closed. Most important, the system is founded on the premise that *the primary purpose of economic activity* is to benefit consumers and maximize the creation of wealth (regardless of its distribution domestically or internationally).

This statement, although made in the specific context of the United States, is even more relevant for countries that attempt to "manage" their economic development with active industrial policies. It shows clearly the potential scope of government actions as the government is called upon to "make" competitive markets exist, if needed, and that undesirable economic activities should be specifically "forbidden." Perhaps even more importantly, it assigns a basic purpose to economic activity, with the state supposed to monitor adherence to it. Arguing on similar lines, Doz (1986: 226) has noted that government intervention "creates both constraints and opportunities, and also modifies the relative attractiveness of various options." Additionally, governments influence the evolution of industry structures and the level of competition, so that policy factors gain critical importance for formulating and implementing business strategy (Doz 1986).

Michael E. Porter (1990) in his seminal study of the competitive advantage of nations has suggested a significant role for government policies in creating competitive advantage for home-based industries. Governments, according to Porter, can influence the developments in both positive and negative ways. Porter therefore suggested that government policy should support domestic firms to "enter new industries where higher productivity can be achieved" (Porter 1990: 618). This view has been supported by Evans (1995: 10) who noted that "[s]tates with transformative aspirations are, almost by definition, looking for ways to participate in 'leading' sectors and shed 'lagging' ones." In the last few decades state interventions with the stated objective of promoting "economic equity and social welfare" have been on the increase (Gilpin 1996). A study of 127 countries by Hall and Jones (1999) found evidence that institutions and government policies are crucial determinants of capital accumulation, productivity, and output per worker.

A similar line of thought has been taken in the academic literature related to "innovation systems," which in addition to private sector players also encompass institutional actors and are affected at national, regional, and sectoral levels by various policy decisions, e.g., by fiscal incentives for conducting R&D, protection of intellectual property rights, labor laws, or by antitrust policies (Freeman 2002; Lundvall 1998; Lundvall et al. 2002; Nelson 1993; Niosi 2002).[4] This is of key importance as the embedded environment consisting of "basic infrastructure and high-tech infrastructure" has been described as "the infrastructure for innovation" and *inter alia* a key determinant for export success by Rasiah (2007). The positive role of improving innovation systems in the success of some industries in Asia (e.g., electronics) has been also highlighted by Ernst (2007), who has exhorted Asian governments to develop suitable policies to upgrade their innovation systems (Ernst 2005).

There is a limit, however, to the role that government policies can play in ensuring competitive advantage and *inter alia* in the development of an industry. In this respect Porter sees only a partial role for the government, noting that government policies alone are not a sufficient source of competitive advantage. According to Porter (1990: 128) "Successful policies work in those industries where underlying determinants of national advantage are present and where government *reinforces* them" (emphasis added). This view is also seconded by the Organisation for Economic Co-Operation and Development (OECD), which recommends that governments should desist from trying to become "main architects" of innovation networks and should instead play a supporting role (OECD 2002). Rasiah and Amin (2010: 289), using Indonesia's case, have argued for a liberal and less interventionist role for the government, suggesting that greater liberalization drives rather than discourages "creative destruction."

Porter (1990) recommended that government be seen as an important variable that affects the competitive advantage of an industry not directly but by influencing the national environment in which it operates. The national environment, in Porter's "Diamond" model, is characterized by a country's given factor conditions, demand conditions, industry structure, and the condition of related and supporting industries. Some of the typical instruments employed by governments to influence the national environment are currency devaluation, deregulation, tax reforms, fiscal incentives, public procurement, and government investments in R&D.

Framework for Policy Analysis
Based on the discussion above, the role of policies may perhaps be succinctly summarized in the words of Peter B. Evans (1995: 9): "emergence of advantage depends on a complex evolution of competitive and cooperative ties among local firms, on government policies, and on a host of other social and political institutions." In the following, the role of government policies is assessed in conjunction with other institutional actors.

For the purpose of this paper, a slightly modified Diamond model, based on Michael E. Porter's, is applied to classify the impact of individual policy measures on the development of the automobile industry (Figure 1). The model ignores the impact of "chance" (Porter 1990:

Figure 1. A Slightly Modified Diamond Model Based on Porter (1990)

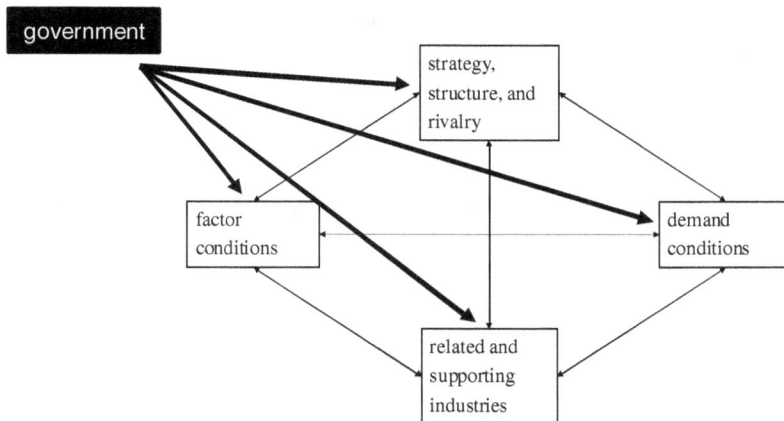

124–126) and concentrates on deliberate policy decisions taken by the government that directly affect the determinants of national advantage in a given industry (Porter 1990: 126–128).

The individual components of the Diamond, in turn, are based on several other factors, such as endowments of human and physical resources, knowledge assets, institutional infrastructure, presence of demanding and sophisticated buyers, size of home demand, presence of internationally competitive related and supporting industries, and strong domestic rivalry between firms that induces strong competition and incentives to innovate (Porter 1990: 69–159). Some early roots of this model can be traced back to studies of innovation diffusion by Griliches (1957), of export advantages by Linder (1961), and of product life cycles by Vernon (1966). It has found broad support in the literature related to "lead markets" and has been applied in adapted forms in various studies (such as Beise 2004; Beise and Cleff 2004; Jänicke 2005; Rennings and Smidt 2008). Porter himself used this model, among others, to explain the success of the Japanese automobile industry (Porter 1990: 161).

The Diamond components are affected by government regulations and policies in various realms such as education and training, R&D investments, antitrust policies, and public procurement (Jänicke and Jacob 2004; Odagiri and Goto 1993; Porter 1990: 625–671).

Evidence of Policy Influences in the Automobile Industry

Most countries are known to have attempted at some point in time or other to "manage" developments in their industries (Doz and Prahalad 1980; Porter 1990: 619). For example, European countries posed restrictions on U.S. capital in the form of high tariffs and discriminatory taxation in the interwar period to protect domestic automobile industries, and the U.S.-Canada Automotive Products Agreement of 1965 was reportedly designed in a way that it "effectively prevents European or Japanese firms from supplying the whole North American market from an assembly plant located either in Canada or the United States without paying import duties" (Jenkins 1987: 14, 32). Spain, in the 1970s, set explicit and tough conditions regulating domestic sales and demanding high export volumes before allowing Ford to establish production facilities in the country (Doz and Prahalad 1980). Some others, for example Japan, have tried in the past to create a favorable scale-enabling industry structure by "encouraging" certain local firms to merge while disallowing FDI (Jenkins 1987: 39; Odagiri and Goto 1993). Yet others may be motivated plainly by intercountry rivalry. For instance, one of the reasons for the automobile industry development programs in Argentina and Brazil is given by Jenkins (1987: 57) in the following terms: "Given the political rivalry between Argentina and Brazil for influence in the region, it was inevitable that if one developed an automotive industry, the other would soon follow suit."

As Gilpin (1987: 99) has noted, "every state, rightly or wrongly, wants to be as close as possible to the innovative end of 'the product cycle' where, it is believed, the highest 'value-added' is located." This has been specifically true of the automobile industry (Doner 1991; Rasiah 2007, 2009), which is widely regarded as a key industry owing to its extended job effects, e.g., in the form of distribution and service stations and deep linkages with other industries such as iron and steel (Jenkins 1987; White 1971). According to the International Organization of Motor Vehicle Manufacturers (known

> *In 2006 the industry's worldwide turnover was US$1.9 trillion, and it employed more than 50 million people*

by its French acronym OICA), the automobile industry had a worldwide turnover of US$1,889.8 billion in 2006 and provided direct and indirect employment to more than 50 million people (OICA 2010b). According to one report, the worldwide export value of automobile products stood at US$847 billion, which is 7 percent of world merchandise trade, and fuel exports amounted to another US$1,808 billion (WTO 2010). These figures demonstrate amply the motivation of the state to intervene in this industry and follow its own development agenda. The state intervention usually can be categorized in two types: (a) interventions that limit the strategic freedom of firms by setting the "fiscal and regulatory ground rules"; and (b) interventions that limit the managerial autonomy, e.g., by asking multinational corporations to forge joint ventures with local partners (cf., Doz and Prahalad 1980).

The following discussion takes a brief look at policy practices and their impacts in developing countries, using studies by Jenkins (1977, 1987) for Latin America, studies by Doner (1988, 1991), Rasiah

(2009), and Rasiah and Amin (2010) for Southeast Asia, and a study by Rasiah (n.d.) for Brazil, India, and South Africa. Our literature review brought to the fore the employment of the following policy measures utilized in the automobile sector in many instances.

1. *Protection against domestic competition.* Governments sometimes may be tempted to ensure economies of scale to the incumbent players by prohibiting entry to new firms, as in Argentina in 1971, or by restricting the number of models to be produced by an incumbent, as done in Mexico in 1972 (Jenkins 1987: 174). Similar restrictions have been reported from some Southeast Asian nations, such as the Philippines and Thailand, in the past (Doner 1991).

2. *Protection against foreign competition.* Governments, in their desire to create a strong indigenous industry base, may grant protection to domestic firms, e.g., by imposing high tariffs on imports. This move is sometimes also utilized as a tool to attract FDI so that foreign firms may be tempted to get "local" treatment. In the case of FDI, some governments are known to require foreign firms to undertake a "joint venture" with a domestic partner, or to pledge a certain amount of local content (which may be as high as 80–90 percent, or to do both (cf., Doner 1991: 41; Jenkins 1987: 58, 191; Rasiah 2009: 152).

Governments sometimes also ban imports of completely built up (CBUs) vehicles or parts thereof altogether, e.g., due to considerations such as a shortage of foreign exchange reserves. In the postwar period this measure was implemented in the case of the auto parts industry in some Latin American countries, e.g., Argentina, Brazil, and Mexico (Jenkins 1987: 17). This led to the development of a competitive local parts industry, which acted as an important pressure group and could be roped in to enforce local content obligations.

3. *Fiscal incentives.* Countries are known to offer investors concession in freight fares and taxes. According to one estimate, Brazil granted an effective subsidy of 89 cents for each U.S. dollar invested in the automobile industry between 1956 and 1961. Mexico followed a similar policy of subsidies in the range of 50–60 percent in the period 1966–72 (Jenkins 1987: 59). Tariff incentives are generally not sufficient by themselves, if the host country cannot provide necessary volumes and enable economies of scale, as experienced in Argentina in the 1930s. Firms may in that case prefer to pay higher tariffs and pass them on to the customer (Jenkins 1987: 19). Such generous subsidies

and tax exemptions are regarded as a key impetus for the development of the automobile industry in Brazil and Mexico.

4. *Export requirements.* Governments may set export requirements for foreign-owned firms to fulfill certain export quotas as a "compensation of imports" (Mexico), or as a requirement to increase the quota for domestic sales (Argentina) in the 1970s. Export promotion was sometimes also coupled with financial incentives, e.g., in the form of tax credits and subsidies. In Argentina, "the total incentive received by an exporting company by 1973 could amount to almost 60 percent of the export price for cars and 75 percent for heavy trucks" (Jenkins 1987: 190–195). Export commitments were also demanded from foreign firms in several Southeast Asian countries (Doner 1991).

5. *Limits on vehicle manufacturers on producing parts in-house.* Governments may restrict the extent to which vehicle manufacturers are allowed to produce parts in-house. Legislation to this effect was introduced in Brazil and Mexico thereby creating a "substantial market for the auxiliary industry" (Jenkins 1987: 63). On the one hand this restriction required local parts producers to upgrade their technological capabilities and to supply more complex parts. On the other hand, in many instances, vehicles manufacturers "persuaded their home country suppliers to follow them into overseas markets." This led to the establishment of a sophisticated auto parts industry, producing under foreign ownership or under license. On the flip side, however, a large number of small-size local producers were left to cater to the replacement market.

6. *Encourage usage of alternative technologies.* In the 1970s, after the oil price crisis, the Brazilian government attempted to "force the companies to develop and produce in growing proportions, alcohol-fuelled vehicles" (Jenkins 1987: 195).

7. *Policies for technology upgrade.* Since technology is considered to be a key, if not *the* key, "driver of long-term productivity growth" (Rasiah 2009: 153), governments on many occasions have tended to offer fiscal incentives for technology upgrades. For instance, Brazil in the 1970s offered "a number of special tax incentives and exemptions from restrictions on import" on imported equipment (Jenkins 1987: 193). However, Rasiah, using Malaysia's example, has proved that protectionist industrial policies have had an adverse impact on the development of firm-level technological capabilities (Rasiah 2009).

Table 1. Government Policies and Their Potential Influence on the Diamond Components

Policy	Impact on the Diamond Components			
	Factor Conditions	Demand Conditions	Strategy, Structure, and Rivalry	Related and Supporting Industries
Protection against domestic competition			X	X
Protection against foreign competition			X	X
Fiscal incentives	X	X	X	X
Export requirements	X		X	X
Limits on producing parts "in-house"			X	X
Support alternative technologies	X	X		X
Policies for technology upgrade	X	X	X	X

Table 1 summarizes these policy factors and their potentially significant impact on the individual components of the national Diamond as defined by Porter (1990). Components are naturally interrelated, and the impact on any one factor naturally influences the others in some way or other.

The table demonstrates that policy measures implemented by governments in some developing economies with regard to the automotive industry have generally focused on the strategy, structure, and rivalry within the industry as well as on the related and supporting industries.

Profile of the Indian Automobile Industry

The Indian automotive industry, which comprises vehicle manufacturers (original equipment manufacturers, or OEMs) and the auto-component industries, is one of the largest industries in India.[5] It has been witnessing impressive growth since the initiation of the country's economic liberalization in the early 1990s. Rising demand owing to the strong growth of the Indian

The automotive industry is one of the largest in India

Table 2. General Classification of Automotive Vehicles in India

Vehicle types		Segments
Four-wheelers	passenger vehicles (PVs)	passenger cars utility vehicles (UVs)
	commercial vehicles (CVs)	light commercial vehicles (LCVs) medium commercial vehicles (MCVs) heavy commercial vehicles (HCVs)
Three-wheelers		passenger carriers goods carriers
Two-wheelers		scooters and scooterettes motorcycles mopeds electric two-wheelers

economy has fuelled this trend. Indian consumers have at their disposal a broad array of automobile models to choose from. The industry produces nearly all kinds of vehicles, which are broadly categorized in Table 2.

In contrast to the 4.8 million units produced at the turn of the millennium in fiscal year 2000–01, the production of vehicles in the country passed a historic milestone of 14 million units in fiscal year 2009–10. India is currently the world's second largest market for two-wheelers (IBEF 2010) and is considered to be one of the fastest growing passenger car markets (GOI 2006a). In 2009, India ranked eighth in the production of commercial vehicles (CVs) and seventh in the production of passenger cars worldwide, moving up

India is the world's second largest market for two-wheelers and is one of the fastest growing passenger car markets

from ranks of thirteenth and fifteenth, respectively, in the year 2000 (OICA 2009, 2010a). Table 3 shows the growth in the production of four-wheelers between 1999 and 2009 in selected economies and reveals that, among major producers, only China has surpassed India on this score.

Table 3. Growth in the Production of Four-wheelers in Selected Economies, 1999–2009

Country	1999 (units)	2009 (units)	Compounded Annual Growth Rate (%)
Argentina	304,809	512,924	5.3
Brazil	1,350,828	3,182,617	8.9
China	1,829,953	13,790,994	22.4
Germany	5,687,692	5,209,857	-0.9
India	818,193	2,632,694	12.4
Indonesia	89,007	464,816	18.0
Japan	9,895,476	7,934,516	-2.2
Malaysia	254,090	489,269	6.8
Mexico	1,549,925	1,561,052	0.1
South Africa	317,367	373,923	1.7
Thailand	322,761	999,378	12.0
United States	13,024,978	5,708,852	-7.9

Sources: Based on OICA (2000, 2010a).

The annual turnover of the Indian automobile industry reached US$38.24 billion in fiscal year 2008–09, up from US$22.9 billion in 2004–05 (SIAM 2010b). Similarly, the annual turnover of the Indian auto-component industry increased more than fivefold, from less than US$4 billion in fiscal year 1999–2000 to US$22 billion in 2009–10 within a span of ten years (ACMA 2010b). Not surprisingly, the automotive industry with its deep backward and forward linkages in the economy has been identified by the Government of India as an important industry with a high potential to increase the share of manufacturing in gross domestic product, exports, and employment (GOI 2006b).

Increased competition on the home turf, together with the growing acceptance of their products in the foreign markets, has encouraged

Table 4. Domestic Sales Trend by Vehicle Type in India, 2003–10				
Fiscal Year	**PVs**	**CVs**	**Three-wheelers**	**Two-wheelers**
FY 2003–04	902,296	260,114	284,078	5,364,249
FY 2004–05	1,061,572	318,430	307,862	6,209,765
FY 2005–06	1,143,076	351,041	359,920	7,052,391
FY 2006–07	1,379,979	467,765	403,910	7,872,334
FY 2007–08	1,547,985	486,817	364,703	7,248,589
FY 2008–09	1,552,703	384,194	349,727	7,437,619
FY 2009–10	1,949,776	531,395	440,368	9,371,231
Sources: Based on SIAM (2010b).				

Indian auto manufacturers to upgrade their technological capabilities through in-house research and development efforts as well as through other means of technology acquisition. For example, the world's cheapest car, unveiled by India's Tata Motors, has received attention from auto manufacturers around the world. The Indian automotive industry with its large number of domestic and foreign players is operating in terms of the dynamics of an open market. The growing installed capacity of the industry reached a figure of

The world's cheapest car has received attention from auto manufacturers around the world

3.88 million four-wheelers and 14.31 million two-and three-wheelers in the year 2009–10 (SIAM 2010b). The competitive conditions within the industry have substantially benefited Indian consumers, who now have access to a wide variety of vehicles with affordable price tags.

Domestic Sales

The Indian automobile market provides a strong and increasing demand base for the growth of the automotive industry. Table 4 shows the domestic sales trend for different vehicle types from the year 2003–04 to 2009–10. As seen in the table, the sale of two-wheelers dominates the Indian automobile market, which can be attributed to the country's poor mass transport system and the need for cheaper and more efficient means of individual mobility (Bajaj Auto 2007).

Another striking characteristic of the market is the rapidly growing demand for PVs and commercial vehicles (CVs). These segments grew at compound annual growth rates (CAGRs) of 13.7 and 12.6 percent, respectively, between 2003–04 and 2009–10. In value terms, the market for PVs and CVs exceeds that of the two-wheelers (GOI 2006a). Further, a look by subsegments into the demand for each of the vehicle segments gives an idea about the preferences of Indian consumers. For instance, in the two-wheelers category, sales of motorcycles currently exceed those of any other subsegment. Similarly, in the PVs category, the sales of small cars (mini and compact) dominate other subsegments (see for instance SIAM 2008c). Such a nature of demand specific to Indian consumers is explained by the country's demographic factors (e.g., highest number of people below the age of 35 years) and socioeconomic factors (e.g., rising middle class). The low rate of ownership of vehicles at present and the presence of strong demand drivers have made India an attractive automobile market (ACMA 2007; GOI 2006a; IBEF 2008).

The low rate of ownership and the presence of strong demand make India an attractive automobile market

The market for auto-components in India has grown along the lines of the automobile market. The domestic sales and imports of auto-components serve the rising demands of both the original equipment manufacturers (OEM) and the replacement market. The increasing number of vehicle models being introduced in the country combined with shorter product life cycle have meant a growing Indian auto-component market, not only in size but also in terms of product diversity (Tiwari et al. 2009). Figure 2 shows the size of the Indian auto-component market over the years from 2003–04 to 2009–10.

The Indian auto-component market has witnessed steep growth. It expanded at an impressive CAGR of over 20 percent between 2003–04 and 2009–10. This growth can be accounted for by increase in both the domestic sales (a 17.8 percent CAGR) and the imports (a

Figure 2. Size and Composition of India's Auto-components Market, 2003–09

US$ billion

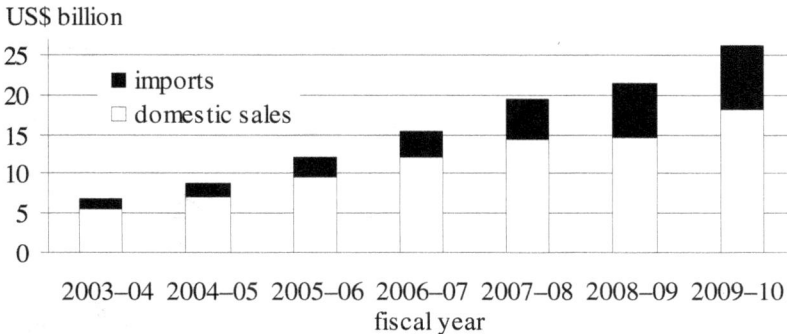

Sources: Data for 2003–04 to 2007–08 are from Ranawat and Tiwari (2009). Other data are calculated from ACMA (2010a).

29.7 percent CAGR) of auto-components. While growth in domestic sales of auto-components could be understood by the general trends in the Indian automobile industry, the growth in imports could possibly be explained by (a) the progressive reduction of import tariffs on auto-components and semi knocked-down (SKD) and completely knocked-down (CKD) kits of automobiles, and (b) newly established foreign automobile manufacturers commencing their operations by assembling SKD/CKD kits.

India's Trade in Automotive Products
According to WTO data, India in previous years has had a positive trade balance in the trade of automotive products, as seen in Figure 3. These figures, however, do not include data for two-wheelers (cf., WTO 2009: 162).

The Indian automotive industry has been registering healthy growth in terms of exports. The share of exports in industry turnover is reported at around 24 percent (GOI 2006b). The export of transportation equipment across all categories increased nearly

The share of exports in industry turnover is around 24 percent

fourteenfold within a span of 10 years, from US$761.8 million in 1998–99 to US$11.15 billion in 2008–09 (RBI 2010). India exports

Figure 3. India's International Trade in Automotive Products, 1998–2009 (US$ million)

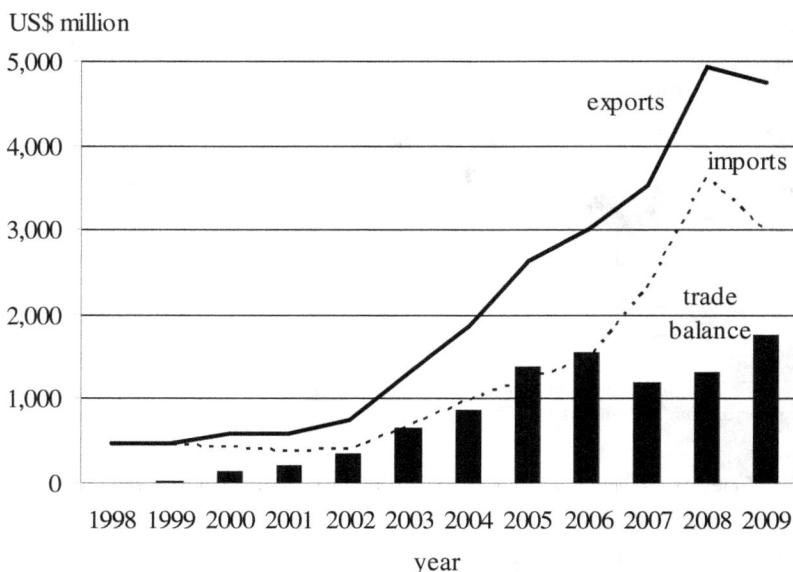

Sources: Based on various annual reports of *International Trade Statistics* by WTO.

both automobiles and auto-components to markets around the world. The key destinations include South Asian neighbors, the European Union (especially Germany, the United Kingdom, Belgium, the Netherlands, and Italy), the Middle East, and North America (GOI 2006a). Increasing pressure in the global competition to source from low-cost countries, combined with the skills and quality advantages of India, is the commonly cited explanation for the growth in India's automotive exports (see for instance Singh 2004).

The exports grew at a CAGR of 22.9 percent for PVs, 17.1 percent for CVs, 16.8 percent for three-wheelers, and 27.5 percent for two-wheelers for the period 2003–04 to 2009–10, despite the global financial crisis in 2008 and 2009. Both domestic and foreign automobile manufacturers have been instrumental in such growth, by making either direct or indirect exports. The domestic manufacturers are forging partnerships with foreign

Exports grew despite the global financial crisis in 2008 and 2009

Figure 4. India's Exports by Vehicle Type, 2003–09

number of units

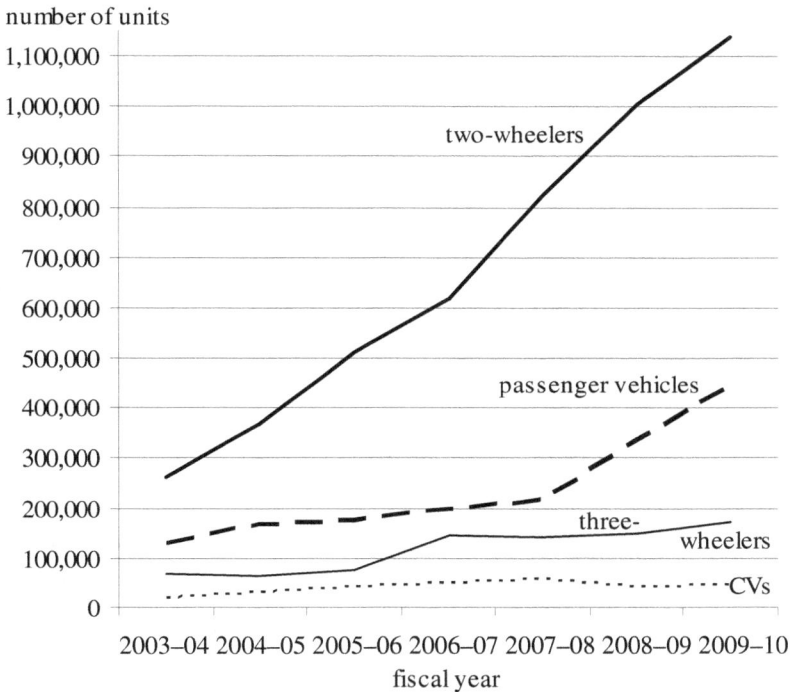

Sources: SIAM (2008b, 2010b).

players or are making outward foreign investments for developing and strengthening their sales overseas (Tiwari and Herstatt 2010). On the other hand, several foreign manufacturers have made India a manu-facturing base for some of their products meant for regional or global exports (IBEF 2005; Tiwari et al. 2009). All this testifies to the fact that the "Made in India" brand is gaining increasing acceptance in the global export markets. Figure 4 shows the export trend of different vehicle types between 2003–04 and 2009–10.

With regard to the Indian auto-component industry, the export performance has been even better. Figure 5

The Indian auto-component industry has established a cost-competitive and quality-conscious image in the global auto industry

Figure 5. India's Exports of Auto-components, 2003–09

US$ billion

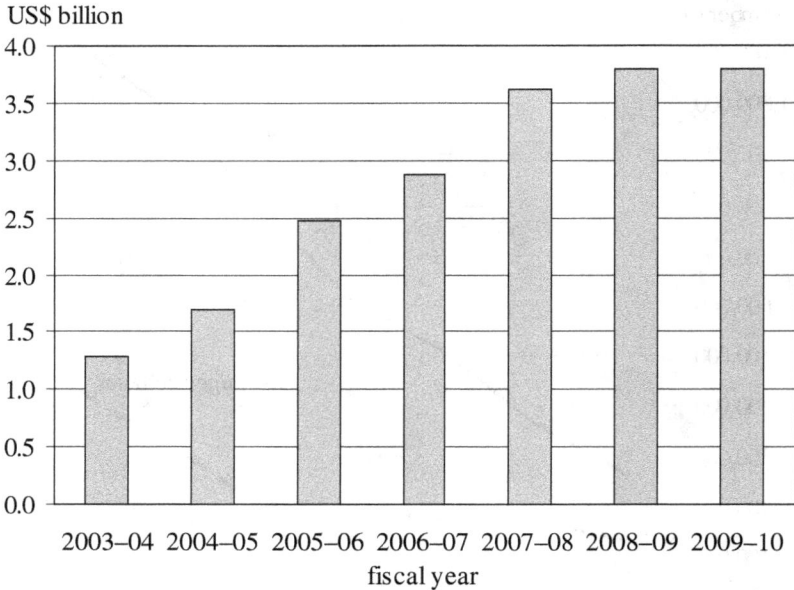

Sources: ACMA (2008b, 2010b).

shows the export trend of auto-components from India over the years 2003– 04 to 2009–10. As seen in the figure, the exports of the Indian auto-component industry grew at an impressive CAGR of 20 percent (valuewise) over the period 2003–04 to 2009–10. The improvement in export performance is also reflected in the shift in the composition of the customer base for exports by the industry. In fiscal year 2009–10, India shipped 80 percent of its auto-component exports to global OEMs and Tier-1 suppliers and 20 percent to the aftermarket, in contrast to 35 percent and 65 percent, respectively, in the 1990s (ACMA 2008a, 2010b). (Tier-1 suppliers are companies that supply the OEMs directly with auto-components, invoicing them directly.) Such a shift has manifested itself in several foreign OEMs and Tier-1 suppliers establishing purchasing offices or subsidiaries in India for the purpose of component sourcing.[6]

Also, foreign OEMs and suppliers are increasingly integrating the Indian auto-component manufacturers into their global sourcing strategies. All this testifies to the fact that the Indian auto-component industry has been able to establish a cost-competitive and quality-conscious image in the global auto industry. With the continuing trend of global outsourcing, the exports of the Indian auto-component industry are estimated to reach US$25 billion by 2015 (ACMA 2008a).

Research and Development

In India's automotive industry, both domestic and foreign automotive firms are undertaking some form of R&D in either their formal or informal R&D units. Most of the R&D efforts of the domestic automotive firms are directed toward value engineering or tweaking the designs to improve performance. The domestic automotive firms have primarily been relying on the foreign partners for product and process technologies, with R&D efforts mainly employed to adapt the designs for in-house production and local demand conditions. However, the threats and opportunities brought about by globalization—e.g., in the form of receding stickiness of knowledge to certain geographies (Ernst 2002) and due to knowledge spillover effects in global production networks (Ernst and Kim 2002)—have encouraged the domestic auto firms to develop core R&D skills (Knowledge@Wharton 2005).

The domestic automobile firms are now increasing their R&D spending on in-house product design and development (Yee 2007). This is evident from the indigenous product development efforts undertaken by the domestic firms (Pradhan and Singh 2009). Tata Motors launched India's first indigenously developed car, the Indica, in 1999 (cf., Nath et al. 2006). Subsequently, commercially successful models (such as the Tata Indigo, Mahindra Scorpio, TVS Scooty, Bajaj Pulsar, and Tata Ace) have been indigenously

> *Tata Motors launched India's first indigenously developed car, the Indica, in 1999*

developed and introduced by the domestic firms (ACMA 2008a). The success of the indigenously developed products has instilled higher confidence in the domestic firms with regard to the development of core R&D capabilities. Nevertheless, the domestic automotive firms "still spend a relatively low amount on R&D as a percentage of sales" (Knowledge@Wharton 2005), compared with the global auto majors.

The investments made by foreign automotive firms in India have primarily been market-seeking (Singh 2004). Rasiah (n.d.) has underscored the role of India's large domestic market as a driver of technology up-grading. R&D efforts undertaken by foreign automotive firms in India have generally been directed to adapt the proprietary designs to Indian market conditions. However, the foreign firms are gradually realizing the attractiveness of India for carrying out their offshore R&D activities (Herstatt et al. 2008; TIFAC 2006). Low-cost scientific talent, grow-ing information technology (IT) skills with sound automotive domain knowledge, and a strong base for prototyping, testing, and validating

> *Foreign firms are gradually realizing the attractiveness of India for carrying out their offshore R&D activities*

auto-components are some of the fac-tors that are furthering such a trend (ACMA 2007). Moreover, the charac-teristic demand of Indian consumers for low-cost and fuel-efficient means of transport, especially small cars, is compelling the global auto majors to undertake product development in India for the purpose of acquiring a new set of capabilities. Such a consid-eration is driven by the global trend in shift from big cars to small cars due to recessionary trends and rising fuel costs. Of late, there have been instances of Indian OEMs and component suppliers also making for-eign direct investments (FDI) abroad in order to seek state-of-the-art technologies. Some noteworthy examples include investments by Tata Motors, Mahindra and Mahindra, Bharat Forge, and Motherson Sumi (Pradhan and Singh 2009; Tiwari and Herstatt 2010).

The policies and programs of the Indian government have also played an important role in stimulating the R&D efforts of the industry. Apart from providing fiscal and monetary incentives for firm-level R&D ac-tivities, the government is playing an active role in the development of common R&D infrastructure. In the year 2005, the government along with industry players launched an initiative for the establishment of world-class testing, homologation, and certification facilities, along with nine R&D centers under the National Automotive Testing and R&D Infrastructure Development Project (NATRiP) (GOI 2006a; Nath et al. 2006). The purpose of NATRiP, established at a total cost of US$388.5 million is to enable the industry "to usher in global standards of vehicu-lar safety, emission and performance standards" (INTEC 2007: 7). To give an example, recently the government has announced financing of a plan of the Automotive Research Association of India (ARAI) to set up advanced laboratories with the purpose of developing less polluting Euro 5 and 6 technologies under NATRiP (*Economic Times* 2011).

Industry Structure

The competition in India's automotive industry has become more intense with the growing number of domestic and foreign firms operating in its automobile and auto-component sectors. The liberalization of the automotive industry in the early 1990s in tandem with the country's favorable macroeconomic trends has contributed to such a development. The entry of foreign firms into the industry has been further encouraged by the advancements in India's foreign investment and trade policies. The cumulative inflows of FDI in India's automotive sector amounted to US$5.13 billion by November 2010 (GOI 2010). It is the seventh largest recipient of FDI with a share of 4 percent in the total inbound FDI. The rising trend of FDI in India's automotive industry depicted in Figure 6 testifies to this fact. Furthermore, fiscal year

Figure 6. FDI in the Indian automotive industry, 2004–09

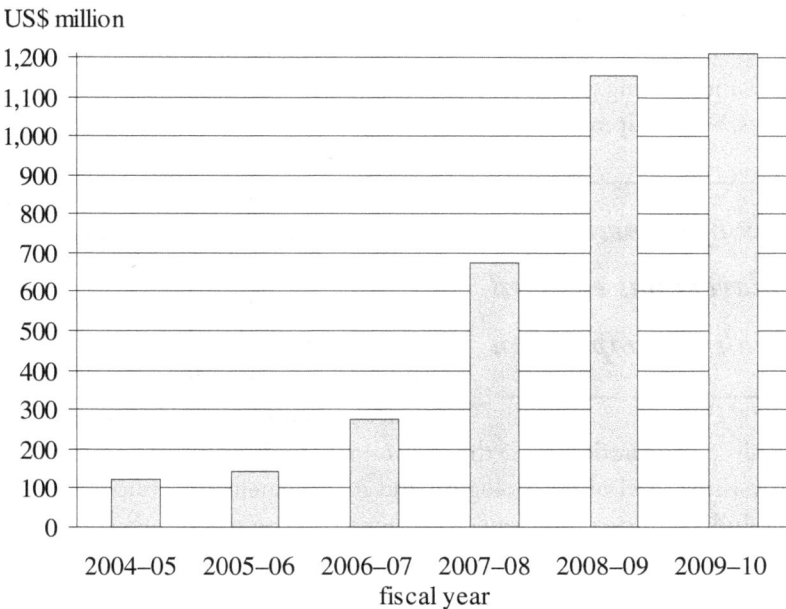

US$ million

Sources: GOI (2008a, 2010).

2010–11 in the period April to November witnessed inflows worth US$533 million (GOI 2010).

The automobile industry in India comprises domestic as well as foreign players. Most of the domestic firms were established in the pre-liberalization period and are currently operational in more than one vehicle segment. In the case of foreign firms, the entries into the Indian market were mainly observed after the year 1993. Firms like Suzuki and Yamaha, which had established joint ventures with Indian partners in the preliberalization period, acquired majority stakes in their ventures subsequently. Among different vehicle segments, the foreign players are predominantly concentrated in the passenger car and CV segments. Thus, a good mix of seasoned domestic players and renowned foreign players has ensured healthy competition in the Indian automobile industry. The automobile models produced by the industry fill up nearly all the price points, addressing varied consumer preferences and thereby further stimulating industry growth. The market shares of key players in different segments of the Indian automobile market for the year 2008–09 are presented in Figure 7.

The Indian auto-component industry comprises around 500 firms in the organized sector and more than 10,000 firms in the unorganized sector (GOI 2006a). The diverse firms produce a comprehensive range of auto-components, which include engine parts, drive transmission and steering parts, body and chassis parts, suspension and braking parts, and equipment and electrical parts (ACMA 2008a). In line with

A good mix of domestic and foreign players has ensured healthy competition

the global trend, the auto-component industry in India has also undergone tierization, with Tier-1 suppliers at the apex and unorganized players at the base of the supply pyramid. For meeting the present day challenges of lean and responsive supply, the auto-component manufacturers in India work in close cooperation with their customers both at home and abroad. The rising level of technological and management capabilities among the Indian auto-component manufacturers have made such collaboration possible.

As in the case of the automobile industry, the structure of the Indian auto-component industry also exhibits a good mix of domestic

Figure 7. Market Shares of Key Players in the Indian Automobile Market, 2008–09

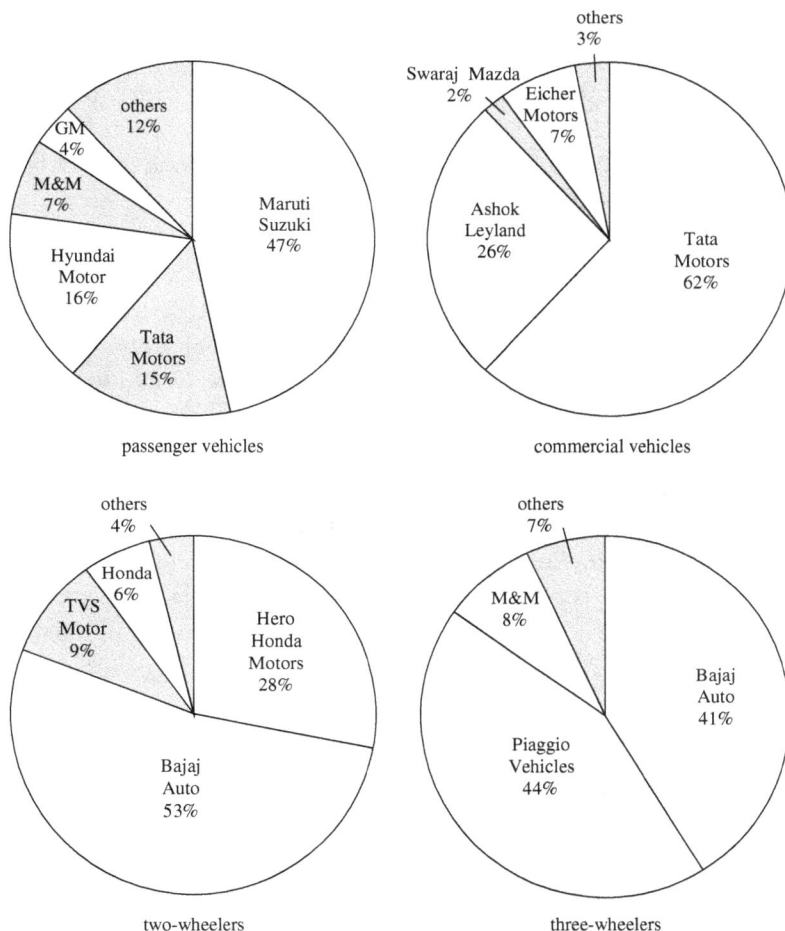

passenger vehicles

- others 12%
- GM 4%
- M&M 7%
- Hyundai Motor 16%
- Tata Motors 15%
- Maruti Suzuki 47%

commercial vehicles

- others 3%
- Swaraj Mazda 2%
- Eicher Motors 7%
- Ashok Leyland 26%
- Tata Motors 62%

two-wheelers

- others 4%
- Honda 6%
- TVS Motor 9%
- Hero Honda Motors 28%
- Bajaj Auto 53%

three-wheelers

- others 7%
- M&M 8%
- Piaggio Vehicles 44%
- Bajaj Auto 41%

Sources: Based on IBEF (2010).

and foreign players. Prominent domestic players in the industry are generally organized as group companies. Some of these auto-component powerhouses are promoted by Indian OEMs themselves. In general, most of the domestic players in the industry have some form of technological collaboration with their foreign counterparts. Further, the entries of foreign OEMs into India have been accompanied by the entries of their existing suppliers, which entered into joint ventures with Indian partners or established subsidiaries, or did both. On the other hand, several foreign auto-component firms have voluntarily entered the subcontinent to cater to the growing demand of the Indian automobile industry.

The growing potential for exports is making the auto-component companies in India increase their production capacities (ACMA 2008a). As a result, the investment in the industry rose from US$2.3 billion in 2001–02 to US$9 billion in 2009–10, growing at a CAGR of around 18.6 percent over the period (ACMA 2010b).

Government Influence on the Automobile Industry in India

Improving investment conditions since 1991 and the changing scenario of global competition have attracted the world's major auto manufacturers into India. Be it market-seeking or low-cost sourcing, India has emerged as an attractive automotive location to offer (global) automotive sector firms strategic advantages. The Indian government has paid special attention to investment and growth within the industry, and its policies have shaped the industry in significant ways.

For instance, the import of automobiles as completely built units (CBUs) generally attracts high customs duties in India. Even though the import duties have been progressively reduced, they are probably still high enough to discourage a significant market for imported CBUs. For example, the total value of imported CBUs in the year 2009–10 was a mere US$267.37 million, compared with the US$38 billion of production within the country.[7] Thus, several foreign automobile manufacturers attracted by the growth prospects of the Indian market have resorted to setting up production facilities in the country. The resulting increase in industry competition and the availability of world-class technology products have further stimulated the domestic demand.

Increased competition and world-class technology have stimulated domestic demand

The evolution of India's automotive industry, seen from a regulatory perspective, has occurred in four phases. The first phase stretched from 1947 to 1965 and was characterized by protectionist policies and an emphatic thrust on indigenization. The second period (1966–79) saw India tighten its regulatory regimes owing to severe domestic economic problems. The third phase (1980–90) saw some relaxation in the regulatory policies, whereas the fourth phase initiated in 1991 has progressively liberalized the regulatory regime (Ranawat and Tiwari 2009).

Policies in the First Phase, 1947–65

After gaining independence from British colonial rule in 1947, India decided to follow an economic model of "mixed economy," which implied that the state retained a significant say in matters related to "what to produce," "how to produce," and "how to distribute" (Ranawat and Tiwari 2009). The Industrial Policy Resolution (IPR) of 1948 placed the automotive industry in the category of "basic industries of importance" whose locations were to be governed by economic factors of national importance, or that required "a considerable investment of a high degree of technical skill" (GOI 2008c: 3). Even though private sector enterprises were free to take initiatives, the state reserved its right to intervene and progressively participate in the industry as and when deemed necessary (Ranawat and Tiwari 2009). In the following discussion, the main areas of policy thrust from the government side in this phase are underlined.

Protection against domestic competition. In pursuance of the IPR of 1948, the Industries (Development and Regulation) Act (IDRA) was promulgated in 1951. The act provided the government with means to implement its industrial policy. While the IPR of 1948 articulated the intentions of the government, IDRA orchestrated the complex implementation of rules and regulations for the planned development. According to the act, "an industrial license was required for a unit with 50 or more workers (100 or more without power) in order to establish a new unit, expand output by more than 5% annually, change location, manufacture a new product, and to conduct business if a change was introduced in policies" (Kathuria 1996: 88). Thus, the IPR of 1948 along with IDRA 1951 created an elaborate licensing system surrounding the Indian industries, including the automotive industry.

In March 1950 the government set up the Planning Commission to oversee the formulation and implementation of India's Five-Year Plans (FYP). The commission had the responsibility of assessing all the resources of the country, augmenting deficient resources, and making plans for the deployment of the resources in the most effective and balanced manner in consideration to the nation's priorities. With respect to the automotive industry, the commission planned the total number of vehicles (per vehicle type) that were to be produced in the given plan period depending on the country's needs and the resources at its disposal. For instance, the first FYP covering the period 1951–56 set a target of raising the production of vehicles in the country from 4,077 in 1951 to 30,000 in 1956 (GOI 1951). Accordingly, the Ministry of Industry administered the capacity licenses issued to the automobile firms.

After the adoption of the Constitution and the integrated socio-economic goals, the industrial policy was revised and adopted in May 1956. Known as the Industrial Policy Resolution of 1956, the revised industrial policy described the "socialist pattern of society" as the objective of Parliament's social and economic policy (GOI 2008b). Accordingly, the IPR of 1956 signaled a higher level of state participation for accelerating industrial development. The resolution grouped the industries into Schedule-A, Schedule-B, and those remaining. Schedule-A industries were either exclusive monopolies of the central government or industries in which any new undertaking was solely reserved for the state. Schedule-B included industries in which the state would establish new undertakings for accelerating future development, and in which the private enterprises had equal opportunity for the same. The remaining industry list, which included the automotive industry, was left to the initiatives and enterprise of the private sector. However, the state reserved its right to participate in the future. Thus, the automotive industry under the IPR of 1956 was provided some autonomy for functioning.

Protection against foreign competition. The IPR of 1948 hinted at the state's disposition of raising tariff barriers for preventing "unfair" foreign competition and for ensuring "judicious use" of the nation's precious foreign reserves. The resolution also proposed central regulation on new foreign investment and stipulated that effective control in future foreign equity collaboration ought to rest in Indian hands. In accordance with the objectives laid down by the IPR of 1948, the Ministry of Industry prepared its first policy for the automotive industry in 1949. As determined in the policy, the tariff on imports of fully built vehicles was raised the same year, virtually banning their import into the country. However, the foreign assemblers assembling CKD vehicles were allowed to continue to operate.

In March 1952, the government referred to the Tariff Commission the question of providing protection and assistance to encourage the automotive industry.[8] The Tariff Commission submitted its report in 1953, recommending that only units with a plan for progressive manufacture of components and complete vehicles may be allowed to operate. Subsequently, foreign assemblers like General Motors and Ford, who considered the domestic demand too low to warrant a local manufacturing program, were obliged to close down their operations within three years. Thus, the exit of foreign assemblers by 1956 and the ban on imports of fully built vehicles since 1949 effectively protected the Indian automotive industry from foreign competition.

> *The exit of foreign assemblers by 1956 and the ban on imports since 1949 protected the Indian automotive industry from foreign competition*

The push for indigenization by imposing a progressive manufacturing program on the automobile firms was in alignment with the overarching goal of "self-reliance" pursued by the then leaders of the nation. At the Tariff Commission's recommendation, a minimum 50 percent indigenous content requirement was introduced. The commission endorsed the already existing manufacturing plan of Hindustan Motors Ltd. (HML) and Premier Automobiles Ltd. (PAL), which had established units for manufacturing some of the components. With the exit of foreign competition, both HML and PAL, which had so far restricted themselves to CVs, embarked on the production of cars. HML had technical collaboration with Morris (United Kingdom) for cars, and PAL with Fiat (Italy) for the same. In addition to these two firms, the manufacturing program of Automobile Products of India, Ashok Motors, and Standard Motor Products for cars and CVs was also approved by the commission. Ashok Motors, established in 1948, renamed itself Ashok Leyland based on its equity collaboration with British Leyland (United Kingdom). Standard Motor Products was in collaboration with Standard Motors (United Kingdom) for the production of cars and CVs. Subsequently, the manufacturing program of one more firm, Mahindra and Mahindra (M&M), was approved for manufacturing utility vehicles (Willys Jeeps).

The second FYP (1956–61) aimed at stepping up the indigenous content of the automobiles to 80 percent by the end of the year 1960–61. Meanwhile by 1956, Tata Engineering and Locomotive Company (TELCO) and Bajaj Tempo entered the industry with programs for CVs. TELCO was in collaboration with Daimler-Benz of Germany, and Bajaj Tempo initially produced three-wheelers under the license of Vidal and Sohn Tempo Werke of Germany. Enfield India, with a program of manufacturing motorcycles, also entered the industry.

Fiscal (dis-)incentives. In order to encourage domestic production and to keep automobile prices low, the government in the early 1950s maintained lower import duties on the components still being imported. However, a steep rise in the prices forced the government to approach the Tariff Commission in 1955. The commission was asked to enquire into and recommend a price policy for automobiles. In its report submitted in October 1956, the commission maintained its initial recommendation against price controls so as not to undermine the development of the industry. It also suggested reviewing the whole question of protection granted to the automotive industry after a period of ten years.

The situation changed soon, however, with the balance-of-payments crisis that sprang up in 1956–57. The ambitious Second FYP with massive outlays on industrial development had strained the nation's foreign reserves. Immediate measures required to counter the economic crisis included cuts on foreign exchange allocated to the automobile manufacturers. Moreover, firms were permitted to produce only one model each. The ensuing reduction in import of vital components compelled the firms to reduce their production. As a result, severe backlogs were generated for the production orders. The decrease in supply of automobiles resulted in steep price increases owing to supply-demand economics. At this juncture, the government decided to impose an "informal price control" on automobiles. This mechanism required the customer to place the order with the dealer and submit a partial payment to the Indian Postal Service. The manufacturer then had to deliver the automobiles in the sequence of the orders registered with the Indian Postal Service. The government also limited the dealer's commission to a maximum of 10 percent and asked the manufacturers to indicate any decision of raising ex-works prices in advance.

Limits on producing parts "in-house." The auto-components in India until the late 1950s had mainly been produced by the in-house manufacturing units of the automobile manufacturers. The requirement of a progressive manufacturing program coupled with the foreign exchange allocation incentives of in-house manufacture resulted in a primarily vertically integrated industry structure. Some large and medium-size auto-component manufacturers, such as L. G. Balakrishnan and Bros. Ltd. and Motor Industries Company (MICO) Ltd., were established during this period with foreign collaboration. The participation of the small-scale sector, however, was limited to the replacement market and to the small jobs from automobile and bigger auto-component manufacturers. This in part could be attributed to the lack of required skills in the small-scale sector and in part to the provisions in foreign collaboration agreements. The latter prevented the larger firms from procuring the components locally, either by explicit clauses or by giving too small concessions on content not procured from the foreign collaborators.

However, the performance of the automotive industry (especially passenger cars) throughout the 1950s had been unsatisfactory. The growing criticism about the quality and price of the automobiles made the government appoint the L. K. Jha Committee to look into these issues. The committee was asked to review the progress of the industry and recommend measures in matters such as reduction of costs. In its report submitted in January 1960, the L. K. Jha Committee observed that the high costs of automobiles were attributable to the neglect and inefficiencies in production owing to the lack of domestic competition. It also noted that the in-house manufacture of components had resulted in an industrial structure devoid of supplier bargaining power, which reduced competition further. In order to reduce costs and improve quality, the committee recommended the encouragement of an indigenous ancillaries sector. The subsequent adoption of these recommendations by the government marked the evolution of a separate auto-component industry in India. Apart from special credit and fiscal concessions, the government came up with protection rates of tariff on a number of ancillary items used in the replacement market. Further, both small-scale units (fixed assets up to 2 million Indian national rupees or INR) and ancillary units (fixed assets up to INR 2.5 million) were exempt from licensing requirements under IDRA (GOI 2008b). Additional encouragement for the small-scale sector came in

1965, with some 60 to 80 components being exclusively reserved for manufacture by the small-scale units following the recommendations of the L. K. Jha Committee. In general, the auto-component industry saw good development during this phase due to the emphasis laid on indigenization within each of the three FYPs.

Commercial vehicles as a priority area. The IPR of 1956 was followed by the introduction of the second FYP (1956–61), which had ambitious programs for rapid development of the industrial sector. Massive investments were planned for the public sector (GOI 1993). The plan targeted a production capacity of 40,000 trucks, 12,000 cars, and 5,000 jeeps for the automotive industry by end of the year 1960–61 (GOI 1956). Greater emphasis was laid on the production of trucks with regard to the nation's priorities in creating an industrial infrastructure that required commercial vehicles for transportation purposes.

In summary, the Indian automotive industry in the years 1947 to 1965 was the one wherein foreign competition was highly restricted by means of protective rates of tariff and foreign investment licensing requirements. Foreign collaboration was permitted only after diligent consideration and was subject to effective control by Indian entities. The domestic competition was also regulated by means of industrial licensing, foreign exchange allocations, and other governmental decrees. The nation's overarching goal of self-reliance was reflected in the indigenization requirements imposed on the domestic automotive firms. Intentions of protecting and nurturing the nascent automotive industry were accompanied by side-effects of high prices and low quality levels. Even though consumer interests were safeguarded to some extent by informal price controls, the overall performance of the industry in terms of quality, consumer choices, and the ready availability of vehicles was unsatisfactory. Further, this phase witnessed the increasing bias of the developmental efforts toward the CV and two-wheeler segment as opposed to passenger cars. With regard to the auto-component segment, the industry structure was largely characterized by in-house manufacturing units and by large and medium-size firms. Efforts to encourage the

> *In the years 1947 to 1965 foreign competition was highly restricted by protective tariffs and licensing*

Table 5. Influence of Policy Factors on Diamond Components in the First Phase, 1947–65

Policy	Impact on the Diamond Components			
	Factor Conditions	Demand Conditions	Strategy, Structure, and Rivalry	Related and Supporting Industries
Protection against domestic competition			X	X
Protection against foreign competition			X	X
Fiscal (dis-)incentives	X	X	X	X
Limits on producing parts "in-house"			X	X
Priority on CVs production		X	X	X

small-scale sector were initiated by the government during this phase. Auto-related institutions—such as the Development Council for Automobiles, the Automotive Component Manufacturers Association of India (ACMA), the Society of Indian Automobile Manufacturers (SIAM), and the Vehicles Research and Development Establishment— also were established during this period. By and large, India seemed to be following policies that were being pursued by other developing nations of that time.

As is evident from Table 5, the Indian government acted in a way similar to most other developing nations by trying to adopt policies that would influence the industry structure and its relations to the related and supporting industries. One major difference, however, is that the government tried to push a specific automotive segment (CVs) in pursuance of its objectives.

Policies in the Second Phase, 1966–79
India's wars with China in 1962 and Pakistan in 1965, along with poor agricultural production due to successive severe droughts, had led to financial crisis in the country by the mid-1960s (cf., Lindblom 1966). The financial situation improved to some extent with the help of a loan

from the International Monetary Fund (IMF) in 1966. However, the formulation and implementation of the Fourth FYP were set aside, and instead three annual plans were drawn up for the period 1967 to 1969. On the political front, the void created by the sudden death of India's fourth Prime Minister in 1966 was filled by Indira Gandhi. Economic and political turmoil deflected the development path of India's automotive industry and strengthened regulatory tendencies.

Fiscal (dis-)incentives. The first change in the automotive policy was initiated in May 1966 with the government directing the Tariff Commission to look into the whole question of the continuance of protection to the automotive industry. The government also asked the Tariff Commission to enquire into the cost structure and fair selling price of different types of automobiles. Although the review was already due, Pinglé (1999: 96) suggests that "the increasingly dominant populist ideology with its anti-big industry emphasis within the political leadership" actually led to the third enquiry. Based on its report submitted in the same year, the Tariff Commission recommended that the government help the industry to attain a minimum efficient scale, by limiting the number of models to an absolute minimum, and impose price controls on passenger cars. Subsequently, the government imposed statutory price controls on passenger cars in September 1969. A court judgment in 1975 quashed them, and later the informal price controls on two-and three-wheelers were also removed.

> *The government imposed statutory price controls on cars in 1969. A court judgment in 1975 quashed them*

Restrictions on economies of scale. Meanwhile, India's first competition law, known as the Monopolies and Restrictive Trade Practices (MRTP) Act, was passed in 1969. The law was intended to check the concentration of economic power in private hands by preventing monopolistic and restrictive trade practices in important economic activities. The MRTP Act classified companies with more than INR 200 million in fixed assets or with a dominant market share of one-fourth or more as "MRTP companies." Such companies were required to obtain additional clearances (apart from those specified by the IDRA) in order to enter, expand, relocate, merge, or acquire. The cumbersome process of obtaining MRTP clearances, which involved public notification of investment plans and semi-public hearings, acted as a deterrent for the companies. Subsequently, the MRTP Commission was set up in 1970 for monitoring monopolistic practices in the industrial sector. Thus, many automotive firms owing to their high levels of investment came under the purview of the MRTP Commission. TELCO was one of the first companies to come under the scrutiny of the commission when it applied to increase its licensed capacity from 24,000 to 36,000 units in December 1970 (Kathuria 1996).

Discouragement of foreign collaboration. Government policies related to foreign collaboration and foreign investment also underwent changes during Indira Gandhi's regime in this period. In the wake of growing criticism regarding the influx of foreign equity collaboration and the dependence on foreign technology, the government appointed the Mudaliar Committee in 1968 to look into foreign collaboration. The stricter approach to foreign equity collaboration recommended by the committee was adopted by the government. Later in 1968, the Foreign Investment Board was established to critically review the acquisition of foreign technology by allowing foreign equity participation. In line with its stricter approach, the government enacted the Foreign Exchange Regulation Act (FERA) in September 1973, consolidating and amending the existing laws on foreign exchange transactions.

With its objective of conserving the country's foreign exchange reserves and ensuring judicious use of them according to national priorities, FERA regulated the import of foreign supplies and the functioning of foreign collaboration. The provisions of the act created additional constraints on the import of technology, raw materials, and components for the industrial sector in general and the automotive industry in particular. The maximum foreign equity participation was brought down to 40 percent under FERA, with exceptions permitted only at the state's discretion. Also, FERA classified companies with more than 40 percent foreign equity as "FERA companies." These companies were subject to greater scrutiny in their operations. Thus, the enactment of MRTP and FERA in the early half of this phase strengthened the regulations surrounding the Indian automotive industry.

Focus on CVs, tractors, and two-wheelers. The Fourth FYP (1969–74) was introduced in 1969. With regard to its policy for automobiles, the government made clear its preference for affordable personal and public transport as opposed to luxurious passenger cars. From an actual production of 35,300 CVs and 84,600 two-and three-wheelers in 1968–69, the fourth FYP set targets of 85,000 and 210,000, respectively, by the end of 1973–74 (GOI 1969). On the other hand, no additional capacity was planned for passenger cars. Between 1970 and 1975, Kinetic Engineering and state-owned Scooters India made their entry into the two-wheeler segment. Kinetic Engineering began producing mopeds, whereas Scooters India commenced production of scooters.

A further setback to the automotive industry came during this phase, with the beginning of the oil crisis in October 1973. The substantial rise in the import bill of crude oil led to a balance-of-payments crisis. The financial woes of the country made the Ministry of Finance and the Ministry of Industry take a closer look at the development of the automobile industry, especially the low fuel-efficiency of Indian automobiles. This led to the division of the automobile industry into luxury (passenger cars) and non-luxury (rest of the industry) segments. The ministries decided to provide encouragement for the growth and technological development of the non-luxury segment, leaving out the luxury segment. Accordingly, CVs were added to the Appendix-I list in 1973, which meant that applications for capacity licenses, foreign collaboration, and so on from the CV manufacturers (including MRTP/FERA companies) were to be treated more favorably.[9] Furthermore, significant capacities were licensed in the two-wheeler segment.

From 1975 onward minor relaxations were made to the licensing regulations. For instance, since 1975 the "automatic growth rule" was applicable to CVs, ancillaries, and tractors. According to this rule, an automatic capacity expansion of 5 percent per year (25 percent in total for five years) was permitted over and above the 5 percent automatic growth permitted under IDRA. Another relaxation, made for non-MRTP and non-FERA automotive firms producing CVs, tractors, ancillaries, and scooters, allowed expansion without limit. However, these relaxations were subject to certain conditions. The product under consideration could not be one reserved for the small-scale sector. Moreover, the requirements of imported machinery, raw-materials, and components arising out of the undertaken expansion required additional clearances. Further, in 1978 the government also dismantled some of its stricter controls on foreign equity collaboration.

Table 6. Influence of Policy Factors on Diamond Components in the Second Phase, 1966–79

Policy	Impact on the Diamond Components			
	Factor Conditions	Demand Conditions	Strategy, Structure, and Rivalry	Related and Supporting Industries
Fiscal (dis-)incentives	X	X	X	X
Restrictions on economies of scale	X	X	X	X
Discouragement of foreign collaboration	X		X	X
Focus on CVs, tractors, and two-wheelers	X	X	X	X
Government support for technology upgrading	X			X

Government support for technology upgrading. The automotive industry in cooperation with the Ministry of Industry established the Automotive Research Association of India in 1966 for supporting R&D efforts within the industry. Additionally, supporting policy measures of the Indian government, such as export-linked fiscal incentives, establishment of export-processing zones, and bilateral or multilateral trade agreements with other countries, have furthered this growth.

Summarizing, it can be argued that government policies in this phase had two major effects on the development of the automotive industry. On the one hand, the industry was shackled by restrictive policies governing antitrust issues and foreign collaboration. On the other hand, the government favored certain industry segments, e.g., two-wheelers, with the intention of making them more affordable for the public at large. Remarkably, India's automotive industry continues to remain strong in some of these segments (tractors and two-wheelers) even today.

This phase, as seen in Table 6, saw a more comprehensive regulatory engagement from the government. Nevertheless, the policy implications reached out also to factor conditions and demand conditions. The government also increased its emphasis on industrial development and public mobility and as a consequence supported segments like CVs, tractors, and two-wheelers.

Policies in the Third Phase, 1980–90
The beginning of this phase was marked with the reelection of Indira Gandhi as the eighth Prime Minister of India in January 1980. The poor performance of Indian industries, exacerbated by the demand problems arising out of unexpected oil shocks of the 1970s, had created resentment about the regulatory policies of the government. As a result, the government thought it necessary to review its existing policies and undertake measures for making the industries more competitive. It therefore decided to ease licensing controls and other restrictive or protective rules governing the industrial sector. It also decided to allow adequate import of technology required for modernization. The Industrial Policy Statement presented in July 1980 gave expression to this shift in government policy.[10] Additionally, the statement emphasized the optimum utilization of installed capacities, the promotion of exports, and regionally balanced economic development. The Sixth FYP (1980–85) introduced in early 1981 reflected these changes in industrial policy. One striking feature of this plan compared with its predecessors was the strong emphasis on exports.

The overall policy shift in the industrial sector brought about important changes within the automotive industry. Various relaxations were made to the regulations pertaining to capacity licensing and foreign collaboration. Imports of capital goods, technology, raw materials, and components required for modernization were also treated more liberally. The encouragement for the development of the CV segment continued in this phase as well. In 1981, the government gave letters of intent to four Indian firms for the manufacture of light commercial vehicles (LCVs). All four firms were in technical-cum-financial collaboration with Japanese players and were licensed a production capacity of 12,500 vehicles per year (Pinglé 1999). The four firms—Swaraj Mazda, DCM-Toyota, Allwyn-Nissan, and Eicher Mitsubishi—commenced their production in 1985.

State participation to spruce-up domestic competition for passenger vehicles. The PVs segment also witnessed a major change during this phase. The policy shift of 1980 intended to favor consumers by providing them with a free choice regarding all types of consumer products, including luxuries. Accordingly, despite being classified in the 1970s as a luxury segment, the passenger car segment was added to the Appendix-I list in 1982 along with UVs and two-and three-wheelers.

Thus, the segment came to be classified as a core industry of national economic importance, whose development was to be favored by the upcoming government policies. Reviewing the development that the passenger car segment had made so far under the existing firms, the government deemed it necessary to increase the competitiveness of the segment by actively participating in it.

Injecting elements of foreign technology and competition. State-owned enterprise Maruti Udyog Ltd. (MUL) entered into collaboration with Suzuki (Japan) in 1982. The Japanese collaborator offered the best deal with three of the latest car models, a 26 percent equity stake, and an indigenization content level agreement of 95 percent by 1988–89. The first car rolled out of MUL's factory in 1984, and with it the face of India's automotive industry changed.[11] Indian consumers, who hitherto had a limited choice of models mostly equipped with outdated technology, were provided with a variety of choices of better-technology and fuel-efficient vehicles in the 1980s. However, the new entry of firms and joint ventures with foreign collaborators witnessed in the period 1982–84 was virtually banned for the rest of the phase, except in the auto-component segment.

Nevertheless, the government also relaxed import regulations to encourage the existing firms to upgrade their technology. Fiscal incentives were provided to the passenger car manufacturers in 1984 to enable them to import technology and improve the fuel efficiency of their vehicles. The domestic firms took advantage of these opportunities and upgraded their technology base, either by direct imports of technology or by foreign equity collaboration. PAL bought a license from Fiat (Italy) for the manufacture of its Fiat 124 model and reengineered it to receive a fuel-efficient Nissan engine produced under license from Nissan (Japan). Similarly, HML purchased the rights to manufacture the phased-out Vauxhall Victor model of Vauxhall Motors (United Kingdom) and modified it to receive a fuel-efficient Isuzu engine licensed from Isuzu (Japan). Sipani Automobiles obtained a license to manufacture the British Reliant Kitten. On the other hand, Standard Motors, which had shelved its passenger car production in the late 1970s, made a bid to reenter the market with a new car model based on the Rover 3500 (United Kingdom) and its own engine.

M&M had enjoyed a monopoly in the UV segment so far. But under the competition from MUL's newly launched UV model, named the Maruti Gypsy, M&M was compelled to upgrade its model with a new Peugeot engine licensed from Peugeot (France). The two-wheeler segment also saw the entry of new players: Kinetic Honda and Hero Honda in collaboration with Honda Motors (Japan) and LML in collaboration with Vespa (Italy). The existing players entered into collaboration with Japanese automotive firms: Bajaj Auto with Kawasaki, TVS Motors with Suzuki, and Escorts with Yamaha. In the face of competition from new Japanese motorcycles, Enfield India introduced new models based on designs bought from Zundapp (Germany).

New players and import relaxations in the early 1980s fundamentally changed the industry

With regard to the CV segment, Ashok Leyland collaborated with Hino (Japan) for new engines. TELCO on the other hand made greater investments in its internal R&D capability. Thus, the entry of new players accompanied by import relaxations in the early 1980s brought about fundamental changes to the structure of the Indian automotive industry.

The auto-component segment also underwent considerable changes during the second half of this phase. The influx of foreign collaboration in the vehicles segment, and thereby ingress of diverse product designs, necessitated technological upgrade from the side of auto-component manufacturers as well. As a result, many domestic manufacturers entered into collaboration with foreign players. Moreover, the foreign collaborators in the vehicles segment were followed by their local suppliers who also entered the Indian market, forging collaboration with the domestic players. Thus, this was the time wherein the Japanese best practices made their way into the Indian automotive industry. Consequently, the insistence on higher quality components and timely deliveries, coupled with the heterogeneous demand, created unrest within the segment. Additionally, the Motor Vehicles Act passed in 1988 mandated the components used in the Indian vehicles to be certified under the standards laid down by the Bureau of Indian Standards.

Enabling economies of scale. In order to make sure that the new automobiles were affordable, the government decided to pay attention to scale economies. It continued its "automatic growth" and "regularization of excess capacity" schemes of the late 1970s. With the addition of all the automotive segments to the Appendix-I list by 1982, the usage of the automatic growth rule became easier for MRTP/FERA companies. Further, the government in 1980 allowed non-MRTP and non-FERA companies in the CV and the two-and three-wheeler segment to expand automatically up to their installed capacities, so as to achieve efficient scale. This was renewed in 1982 as a reendorsement of capacity up to 133 percent of the best production of the previous five years, given that the capacity utilization had partially reached 94 percent. The facility was made available to Appendix-I MRTP/FERA companies as well. For an initial period, the government also lowered the customs duty on imports of components for fuel-efficient vehicles.

In January 1985 the government announced a policy of "broad-banding" encompassing the entire industrial sector, which allowed manufacturers to use the installed machinery flexibly. Under the broad-banding scheme, the production licenses were issued for a broader product group as opposed to the single-product licenses issued previously. The manufacturers were not required to obtain any additional clearances for diversifying within their product groups as long as the diversification did not necessitate any new investment in machinery. The scheme was conceived to liberalize production by providing the manufacturers with freedom to select the right product mix to be produced, and thereby make optimal use of their capital investments.

In 1985, the broad-banding grouped passenger cars, CVs, and UVs into one product group named "on-road four-wheelers." This change meant that any firm operational in the aforementioned segments, within its overall capacity, had the opportunity to diversify into any other segment within the group or to vary the product mix over the segments based on the demand conditions. TELCO seized this opportunity by diversifying into the LCV segment with an indigenously developed model in 1986. It also entered into the UV segment with its pick-up truck in 1988. Similarly, broad-banding grouped all the two-wheelers up to 350cc engine capacity into one group, which was later expanded in 1986 to include three-wheelers. A similar broad-banding group was announced for automobile ancillaries as well. In addition to the broad-banding policy, Rajiv Gandhi's regime also brought some other relaxations. From May 1985, all the automobile and component manufacturers were exempted from sections 21 and 22 of the MRTP Act, which meant that the large industrial houses were no longer required to obtain MRTP approvals. In 1986, the "minimum economic scale" scheme was announced, under which the government promised to actively encourage firms to achieve an economic scale of operations.

The component segment was given due attention since its development was considered critical for the modernization drive. The relaxations pertaining to relatively liberal entry, growth, and imports of foreign supplies were also available to the auto-component segment. The broad-banding product categories for auto-components were quite large, enabling sufficient diversification by the existing players. In March 1985, the auto-component segment was delicensed under IDRA for non-MRTP and non-FERA companies with the condition that the firm was not located within urban or municipal limits. Further, for MRTP/FERA companies the delicensing was applicable for investment in backward areas. Encouragement to the small-scale sector was also continued during this phase, with the government raising the investment limit from INR 1 million to INR 2 million for small scale units and from INR 1.5 million to INR 2.5 million for ancillary units (GOI 2008c).

Export promotion. The fresh economic ideology and political perspective of the new Prime Minister was reflected in the Seventh FYP (1985–90), with its focus on exports and liberalization in industrial production. The export performance of the automotive industry between the years 1951 and 1980 had been mediocre. Being a net user of foreign exchange, the automotive industry was given much attention during the seventh plan period for improving its export performance. Accordingly, various export promotion measures were implemented by the government. As a consequence, exports by the Indian automotive industry nearly doubled from INR 1,561 million in 1984–85 to INR 3,041 million in 1988–89 (ACMA 1991 cited in Chugan 1995).

To summarize, the limited liberalization that took place during this phase had a considerable impact on the development of India's automotive industry. The modernization program of the early 1980s intensified competition in the industry and upgraded its technological

Table 7. Influence of Policy Factors on Diamond Components in the Third Phase, 1980–90

Policy	Impact on the Diamond Components			
	Factor Conditions	Demand Conditions	Strategy, Structure, and Rivalry	Related and Supporting Industries
State participation in car manufacturing			X	
Increased foreign competition		X	X	
Injection of foreign technology	X	X	X	X
Enabling economies of scale	X	X	X	X
Export performance	X		X	X

base. The relaxations in the form of new entries, foreign collaborations, automatic growth, reendorsement of capacity, liberal MRTP/FERA implementations, and broad-banding facilitated in driving the change. The drive for indigenization continued during this phase, with all the vehicle and component joint ventures required under the phased manufacturing program to achieve 95 percent indigenization within five years of the start of production.

In the 1980s, a variety of choices was made available to Indian consumers

Passenger cars, a non-priority sector in the 1970s, came to be identified as a core industry of national importance. Indian consumers, who had hitherto been restricted to a few models with outdated technology, were given a free choice in the 1980s to select among a variety of better-technology and fuel-efficient vehicles, including luxury vehicles.

The third phase saw the continued thrust of policy initiatives on multiple components of the national "Diamond," as outlined in Table 7. In this phase several measures also had a direct influence on demand conditions.

Policies in the Fourth Phase, 1991 Onward

The economic crisis of 1990–91, followed by a major shift in the country's overall economic policy framework (Ahluwalia 2002, 2006), marked the beginning of the fourth phase. Increased governmental expenditure combined with poor performance of the public undertakings had led to growing budget deficits throughout the 1980s. The financial woes of the country were exacerbated by the commencement of the Gulf War in August 1990. The steep hike in the import bill for crude oil coupled with decreasing remittances from Indian expatriates in the Gulf led to a sharp decline in the country's foreign exchange reserves. By the end of 1990, the reserves dropped to levels that were not sufficient for even a fortnight, and there was a serious possibility of default. In January 1991, the government accepted a loan from the IMF's Compensatory and Contingency Financing Facility. Subsequently in July 1991, the new government headed by Prime Minister P. V. Narasimha Rao approached the IMF for another loan. This loan was accompanied by conditions regarding control measures for the budget deficit as well as the implementation of economic structural reforms.

In line with its agreement to the conditions laid down by the international financial institutions, the government adopted a new economic policy in July 1991. The new policy proposed wide ranging economic reforms in an attempt to liberalize and open up the economy. Structural reforms encompassing deregulation of the industrial sector, trade and investment policy reforms, financial sector reforms, tax reforms, and foreign exchange reforms were envisaged for this purpose. Accordingly, a new Industrial Policy Statement was introduced by the government in July 1991. The thrust of the new industrial policy was toward creating a more competitive environment in the sector and removing the barriers to entry and growth of firms. Some important policy decisions made by the government in this regard were as follows (GOI 2008c):

In line with conditions laid down by the IMF, the government adopted a new economic policy in July 1991

- Abolishment of the industrial licensing system for all except a few industries related to strategic and security concerns.
- Automatic approval of FDI up to 51 percent equity in high-priority industries.[12]
- Automatic clearance for imported capital goods with the condition that the foreign exchange required is available through foreign equity.
- Automatic permission for foreign technology agreements in high-priority industries subject to the prescribed royalty rates or a lump-sum payment not exceeding INR 10 million.
- Amendment of the MRTP Act to remove the threshold limit of assets for MRTP companies and large dominant undertakings, which effectively eliminated the need for such companies to obtain any further MRTP clearances.
- Review of the existing portfolio of public investments with greater realism and progressive disinvestment in public enterprises where the private sector had developed sufficient expertise and resources.

The sweeping changes in overall industrial policy had a significant impact on the development course of India's automotive industry. Though a few liberalization measures had already been introduced in the 1980s, the policy reforms initiated in 1991 were much more comprehensive, as described below.

Unshackled domestic and foreign competition. All vehicle and component segments (initially excluding passenger cars) were delicensed in July 1991. The passenger car segment was delicensed in May 1993. Along with abolition of the need for MRTP clearances, this meant that the automotive firms were allowed to enter, expand, diversify, merge, or acquire based on their commercial judgments. The liberalization concerning foreign investment encouraged several global players to enter the Indian market and establish joint ventures with domestic players. FDI up to 51 percent was allowed on an automatic basis, and more than 51 percent was possible with governmental clearance, granted on a case-to-case basis depending on the projected exports, sophistication of technology brought in, and so on. The phased manufacturing program requiring time-bound indigenization was dropped in 1991 for the new units and in 1994 for the existing units.

Fiscal (dis-)incentives. While the aforementioned structural reforms benefited the automotive industry over a longer term, the short-term stabilization measures adopted by the government to counter the crisis adversely affected the industry's growth. As an immediate measure to improve the country's balance-of-payments situation, the government discouraged the consumption of oil by imposing a surcharge of 25 percent on petroleum products. It also imposed a heavy excise duty on the selling price of all automobiles. For instance, the excise duty on passenger cars was increased from 42 percent to 53 percent in August 1990, and further raised to 66 percent in July 1991 (Sumantran et al. 1993). Additionally, in order to reduce the trade deficit the rupee was devalued, and the auxiliary customs duty was increased. The escalation of the yen-rupee exchange rate combined with the increased costs of production of the newer import-dependent components undermined the performance of firms with recent Japanese collaboration. On the demand side, the overall hike in fuel prices and the credit squeeze to curb inflation stifled the demand for automobiles in the country. The change in the allowed rate of depreciation from 33 percent to 20 percent was an additional discouragement for the market (Sumantran et al. 1993).

The automotive industry saw a negative annual growth rate of 10.1 percent in the vehicles segment in the year 1991–92, but recovered in the subsequent years of the postreform period. The excise duty was reduced from 66 percent to 55 percent on passenger cars and from 15 percent to 10 percent on LCVs in June 1992 (Sumantran et al. 1993). The excise duties on other vehicle segments were also rationalized. The tariff structure for auto-related imports also underwent changes, and the peak tariff rate was reduced progressively from 150 percent in 1991 to 110 percent in 1992, 85 percent in 1993, 65 percent in 1994 and 50 percent in 1995 (Kathuria 1996). The tariff rate for capital goods underwent similar reductions. Additionally, the imports and exports were allowed at a market-determined exchange rate. Thus, the lowering of trade barriers, the possibility of making direct investments, and the promising growth potential of the domestic market brought India onto the radar screen of international automotive players.

The passenger car segment, with its high growth potential, saw the most hectic activities from the foreign automotive firms. By the mid-1990s, several foreign players had entered the Indian passenger car market mainly by setting up joint ventures with local firms: Mercedes-Benz with TELCO (1994), General Motors with HML (1994), Peugeot with PAL (1994), Daewoo with acquisition of DCM-Toyota (1995), Honda Motors with Siel Ltd. (1995), Ford with M&M (1996), Hyundai with a 100-percent-owned subsidiary (1996), Fiat with Tata Motors (1997), and Toyota with the Kirloskar Group (1997). In the CV segment, Tata in collaboration with Vectra Motors (1997) and Volvo with its 100-percent-owned subsidiary (1997) made their foray into the Indian market. Most of these new ventures proposed initially only to assemble SKD/CKD kits. As a result, for balance-of-payments reasons the government in 1995 asked these companies to commit individually to an equivalent amount of exports.

By the mid-1990s, foreign players had entered the car market by setting up joint ventures

In 1997, the Ministry of Industry in its policy for automotive industry placed import of capital goods and auto-components under Open General License, but regulated the import of automotive vehicles in CBU form or in SKD/CKD condition. The vehicle manufacturing units were allowed to import vehicles only in SKD/CKD condition and were required to obtain a license for the same. The availability of a license was subject to execution of a memorandum of understanding signed with the Directorate General of Foreign Trade (DGFT). As described in (GOI 2002: 2-3), such a memorandum required the companies to:

- have a plan for actual production and not just merely assemble SKD/CKD kits,
- bring in at least US$50 million for having operations as a subsidiary,
- reach an indigenization content level of 50 percent in the third and 70 percent in the fifth year from the date of clearance of the first lot of imports, and
- neutralize foreign exchange outgo on imports by equivalent exports (beginning in the third year after the start of operations).

Eleven companies had signed such memorandums with the DGFT by April 2001 (GOI 2002). Meanwhile, the passenger car segment saw the entry of Skoda in 1999. In the two-and three-wheeler segment, the trend was for the earlier foreign collaborators of the 1980s either to acquire majority stake in the joint ventures or to establish independent subsidiaries in the country. Accordingly, Yamaha (1995), Piaggio (1998), and Honda (1999) made their independent forays into the Indian market. With the need for being more investor-friendly, subsequent improvements have been introduced into the automotive policy from time to time—for instance in January 2000 by eliminating the requirement of foreign exchange neutrality for new investors. Since April 2001, the SKD/CKD and even CBU imports were put on the Open General License list, thereby eliminating the need for new investors to obtain a license under a memorandum with the DGFT. The quantitative restrictions on imports were therefore effectively removed. The export commitments for the already existing foreign investors were abolished in August 2002.

Along with reductions in the overall tariff level to open up India for international trade, the government has also progressively rationalized its domestic taxation structure. For instance, the peak rate of excise duty on passenger cars has been brought down from 66 percent in 1991– 92 to 22 percent in 2009–10.[13] With regard to the import tariffs in the year 2008–09, the customs duty on WTO-bound segments (CVs and auto-components) has been reduced to 10 percent, whereas that for the WTO-unbound segments (passenger cars, multi-utility vehicles, and two-and three-wheelers) has been 10 percent for CKD units and 60 percent for the SKD/CBU form (SIAM 2008a).

Modernization program with global ambitions. With a vision of establishing a globally competitive automotive industry in India and doubling its contribution to the economy by 2010, the Ministry of Industry presented for the first time a separate auto policy document in March 2002.

> *India is on target to become an international hub for manufacturing small cars*

Known as "Auto Policy 2002," the document superseded the auto policy adopted in 1997 by addressing emerging problems, being more investor friendly, and ensuring compatibility with WTO commitments. Auto Policy 2002 is intended to make the Indian automotive industry globally competitive. It aims at promoting modernization and indigenous design and development within the country as well as establishing domestic safety and environmental standards on a par with international ones. Furthermore, India is on target to become an international hub for manufacturing small cars as well as a key center in the world for two-wheelers and tractors. Accordingly, the policy proposes various initiatives relating to investment, tariffs, duties, and imports in order to achieve these objectives.

Auto Policy 2002 allows automatic approval of foreign equity investment up to 100 percent for the manufacture of automobiles and auto-components. With regard to the tariff structure, the policy proposes to fix import tariffs in a way that the actual production within the country would be facilitated over mere assembly, without providing undue protection at the same time. This was mainly applicable to the WTO-unbound segments (passenger cars, UVs, and two-and three-wheelers).[14] For WTO-bound segments (CVs and auto-components), the policy proposes to encourage the domestic players by providing adequate accommodation for attaining global standards. The thrust for automotive R&D continues in this policy, but with renewed vigor. Suitable fiscal and financial incentives were planned for promoting industry R&D efforts. For instance, a weighted tax deduction of more than 125 percent was decided for the R&D activities of vehicle and component manufacturers (GOI 2002). The policy also plans to increase the allocations to the automotive cess fund created for R&D in the automotive industry and to expand the scope of activities covered under it. Strengthening environmental and safety standards is also stressed in Auto Policy 2002.

Within a decade of introducing structural reforms, production increased significantly

The policies laid down by Auto Policy 2002 have continued to apply up to the present, with minor modifications. Within a decade of introducing structural reforms into the country, the production of India's automotive industry had increased significantly.

Thus, during this phase, the increasingly investor friendly as well as liberal trade measures adopted by the government have led to a momentous increase in the number of foreign players active in the country. The dismantling of licensing controls has also encouraged entrepreneurial endeavors on the part of domestic players. The market for automotive vehicles in India, which had earlier been virtually a seller's market, was transformed into a buyer's market. Indian consumers have benefited from the intensified competition, which has brought their requirements of a cost-effective, technologically competent, fuel-efficient, and reliable means of transport into perspective. The strong drivers of macroeconomic base of demand growth along with convenient credit facilities have ensured rising demand for vehicles in the country. Hence, the bold attempt of the government in making a major shift in its economic policy framework in the early 1990s, along with its continued support to the automotive industry, put the industry on a fast track of development.[15]

With regard to the auto-component segment, the phase witnessed the entry of several foreign auto-component firms, mainly following their global OEM customers into the Indian market. By the end of the year 2000, all major global Tier-1 suppliers had a presence in India. The competition on the home turf, as well as the expanding domestic and international market for their products, spurred the domestic auto-component producers to upgrade their technology and management practices. Further, the cost-effective and quality auto-components produced in India are increasingly gaining acceptance in international markets.

Increased interdependence between Indian and foreign firms is globalizing India's automotive industry

Indian auto-component firms are increasingly becoming integrated into the global supply chains of automobile and auto-component majors worldwide. And the automobiles produced in India are increasingly making their way into foreign markets through either direct or indirect exports. The government has increasingly and actively encouraged Indian firms to engage in outbound FDI and to set up subsidiaries and joint ventures abroad (Bruche 2010; Tiwari and Herstatt 2010). Domestic automobile manufacturers are teaming up with foreign auto-component firms for bringing out new vehicle models. Hence, such increased interaction and interdependence between the Indian automotive firms and their foreign counterparts is leading to increasing globalization of India's automotive industry.

Technological up-gradation. Environmental and safety standards as an integral and important part of the modern automotive industry began to receive some attention during this phase (cf. KPMG 2010). The first state emission norms came into force for petrol vehicles in 1991 and for diesel ones in 1992. Euro I, Euro II, and Euro III norms were subsequently introduced in India in 1996, 2000, and 2005 respectively. Efforts are being made to align Indian safety standards with global ones. With its accession to United Nations Working Party-29 in 2005, India has been making efforts toward the harmonization of auto standards worldwide and therefore integrating its auto industry into the global automotive industry. On the technology front, the liberalization concerning foreign technology agreements and foreign collaboration infused world-class technology into the industry. The government has encouraged efforts for assimilating the latest foreign technology and indigenizing design and development. Fiscal incentives as well as institutional support have been provided for encouraging industry R&D efforts. The domestic R&D efforts came to fruition with the launch of India's first indigenously developed car, the Indica, by Tata Motors in 1999. Over the years, many domestic as well as foreign firms have set up R&D facilities in the country. The importance of the domestic market for technology up-gradation has been highlighted by Rasiah (n.d.: 27), who has held "that exposure to international markets has not made significant differences in the development of technological capabilities in India. The much larger domestic market seems to have provided much more scale appropriation opportunities in India than those of Brazil and South Africa."

Summarizing, it may be said that the liberalization phase has seen India open up its automotive sector considerably with no noteworthy restriction on domestic competition and very few restrictions on foreign competition. One significant exception to this is the continued high import duty on certain CBU categories, such as "[m]otor cars and other motor vehicles principally designed for the transport of persons," which pay a customs duty of 100 percent (SIAM 2010a). The liberalization has made a significant overall contribution to the development and international competitiveness of India's automotive industry.

As evident from Table 8, this phase has seen major policy initiatives which had a comprehensive effect on all components of the "Diamond." In particular, government actions also had a positive effect

Table 8. Influence of Policy Factors on Diamond Components in the Fourth Phase, 1991 Onward

Policy	Impact on the Diamond Components			
	Factor Conditions	Demand Conditions	Strategy, Structure, and Rivalry	Related and Supporting Industries
Liberalization of domestic competition	X	X	X	X
Liberalization of foreign competition	X	X	X	X
Injection of foreign technology	X	X	X	X
Thrust on export of small cars	X	X	X	X
Technological up-gradation	X	X	X	X
Fiscal (dis-)incentives	X	X	X	X

on demand conditions. The government's effort to promote India as a global hub for small cars had a positive correlation with the large and price-conscious domestic market. In this phase, export orientation had a positive impact also on demand conditions, as the government progressively reduced excise duties, which resulted in lower costs also for the domestic market.

Summary and Conclusions

This paper has attempted to identify policies that have had a significant impact on the development of India's automotive industry. The evolution of India's automotive industry occurred in four phases. In the first (1947–65) and second (1966–79) phases, the important policies were related to protection, indigenization, and regulation of the industry. On the one hand, these policies helped India build an indigenous automotive industry, while on the other hand it led to unsatisfactory industry performance. In the third phase (1980–90), the policy thrust was on the infusion of new technology. The foreign competition inducted into the industry transformed its dynamics. Lastly, in the fourth phase (1991 onward) the liberalization with regard to foreign investment has had a significant influence on the Indian automotive industry as seen today.

The study comes to the conclusion that the government played a key role in the evolution of the Indian automobile industry. In the postindependence era, the government was in an overregulation mode, at least to some extent, sometimes motivated by ideological reasons and at other times constrained by fiscal resources, stifling domestic competition, shutting the doors on foreign firms, and even regulating prices. With the benefit of hindsight, it might be argued that protectionist policies followed by the successive governments in the prereform era caused considerable opportunity costs for the Indian automobile industry, for consumers, and for the state itself.

On the other hand, especially in comparison with many other developing nations that gained independence from colonial rule at about the same time, the government has been relatively successful in creating or supporting favorable innovation systems, or doing both, at national, regional, and sectoral levels. With its insistence on indigenization in the prereform era, it has managed to sustain a significant domestic base, which has been able to

The government has been relatively successful in creating innovation systems

withstand the competitive pressure in the postliberalization period and has also even managed to expand overseas.

Foreign automobile sector firms that have invested in India have been largely able to operate without many strings attached and have significantly contributed to the upgrading of the sectoral innovation system. The government has played a proactive role in supporting outward FDI by Indian automotive firms. Of late, there has been considerable support in government circles for product innovations and formal R&D. In particular, the segment of compact small cars has seen fiscal incentives, such as a reduced rate of excise duties, and the government would like to see India emerge as an innovation and production hub for compact cars. Additionally, investments in the basic infrastructure, such as roads and highways, have also provided a boost to the automobile industry.

Two interesting aspects of the government's impact on the development of the automobile industry in India make it appear to be a "benevolent benefactor" at certain times and may be summarized as follows.

First, the Indian government, unlike its counterparts in many other developing nations has not concentrated its attempts singularly on influencing the industry structures or creating local supplier industries. (See the subsection on "Evidence of Policy Influences" above.) Its policy measures especially since the 1990s, to a greater extent than those of some other developing nations, have tried to actively create favorable factor and demand conditions, thereby strengthening the local market and giving a key impetus to the development of the industry.

Second, India put an early focus on some specific segments of the automobile industry. This focus, in a protected environment, gave rise to strong domestic players, who were able to take advantage of the liberalization gradually injected at a later stage. The specialization effects seem to be helping India's industry succeed globally, especially in the two-wheeler and small car segments.

Nonetheless, the government would be well advised to continue the reform process. An enhanced thrust on innovations is required more than ever, in order to upgrade the safety and emission norms while allowing for products affordable for larger sections of the society within the country. While private sector firms, both domestic and foreign-owned, are actively pursuing development and design activities in India, they are often faced with a shortage of skilled and experienced engineers. The government would be well advised to intensify efforts to upgrade India's base of skilled labor, including the blue-collar segment. Raising safety and environmental standards will help reduce negative country-of-origin effects, sometimes associated with products made in India, and provide better access to other global markets, which could potentially see India emerge as a "lead market" for compact small cars.

Endnotes

1. India's fiscal year runs from April of a given calendar year through March of the following calendar year.

2. Government intentions for intervening in industry development are usually articulated in policy forms such as industrial policy, trade policy, fiscal policy, and so on. Torjman (2005: 4) defines policy as "a deliberate and (usually) careful decision that provides guidance for addressing selected...concerns." Policy development is therefore a decision-making process, which generally involves identifying the objective and determining the pathway to the objective, based on criteria such as effectiveness, costs, resources required for implementation, and political context (Torjman 2005).

3. For a discussion of the deeper role of "institutions" in economic development, see North (1989) and Rodrik (2000).

4. For a collection of definitions of National Innovation Systems, see Herstatt et al. (2008: 6).

5. The Indian tire industry had a turnover of US$5.27 billion and exports of US$765 million in fiscal year 2009–10 (ATMA 2011). It can be also considered a part of the Indian automotive industry. The figures have been converted from Indian national rupees (INR) using the average exchange rate in FY 2009–10 of US$1 = INR 47.4166 (RBI 2010). This paper, however, focuses on vehicle manufacturers and parts suppliers and does not include the tire suppliers in its examinations.

6. Some foreign players have established exclusive export-oriented units in India for this purpose. For example, the global Tier-1 supplier Visteon has a 100 percent exclusive export-oriented unit near Chennai in India.

7. The import value was obtained from the Export Import Data Bank (Tariff items 8703 and 8711) of the Directorate General of Foreign Trade (DGFT), Government of India (available at www.dgft.delhi.nic.in).

8. Set up in 1951, the Tariff Commission had the functions of adjusting duties of customs or any other duties in relation to any industry, actions relating to the dumping of goods for imports or otherwise, and granting protection for the

encouragement of industry and action in cases where industry has been taking undue advantage of tariff protection (GOI 2008b).

9. In 1970, the government issued a list of nine core industries (including tractors) that were designated as national priorities. This list, revised in 1973 with the addition of CVs, was colloquially referred to as "Appendix-I."

10. Intermediate to the Industrial Policy Resolution of 1956 and the Industrial Policy Statement of 1980, an industrial policy statement was also introduced by the Janata Party government in 1977. The statement, *inter alia*, placed emphasis on relaxation of import controls and efforts to increase industrial exports.

11. For a brief historical background on Suzuki's engagement with MUL, see Bhargava (2010) and Sahoo (2010).

12. High priority industries, requiring large investments and advanced technology, have generally been known as the "Appendix-I industries." Since 1982, all segments of the automotive industry had been on the Appendix-I list.

13. The excise duty on automotive vehicles and auto-components in the year 2009–10 ranges between 10 percent and 22 percent in general (SIAM 2010a).

14. Unlike WTO-bound goods, WTO-unbound goods do not have a WTO-committed ceiling on the custom duty rates.

15. With the liberalization of the economy and the accompanying de-emphasis of the public sector, the role of the Planning Commission had become less pronounced and mainly of an indicative nature. The role of government for the automotive industry has therefore been that of a facilitator.

Bibliography

Ahluwalia, Montek Singh. 2002. "Economic Reforms in India since 1991: Has Gradualism Worked?" *Journal of Economic Perspectives* 16(3): 67–88.

———. 2006. "India's Experience with Globalisation." *Australian Economic Review* 39(1): 1–13.

Automotive Component Manufacturers Association of India (ACMA). 1991. *Automotive Industry of India: Facts and Figures.* New Delhi: Automotive Component Manufacturers Association of India.

———. 2007. *Indian Automotive Component Industry: Engine of Growth Driving the Indian Manufacturing Sector.* New Delhi: Automotive Component Manufacturers Association of India.

———. 2008a. *Global Competitiveness of Indian Auto Component Industry and Its Sustainability.* New Delhi: Automotive Component Manufacturers Association of India.

———. 2008b. *Industry Statistics: Auto Component Industry (1997–98 to 2007–08).* New Delhi: Automotive Component Manufacturers Association of India.

———. 2010a. *Indian Auto Components Industry: An Overview.* New Delhi: Automotive Component Manufacturers Association of India.

———. 2010b. *Industry Statistics: Industry Statistics at a Glance.* New Delhi: Automotive Component Manufacturers Association of India.

Automotive Tyre Manufacturers Association of India (ATMA). 2011. *Overview of Indian Tyre Industry: Financial Year 2009–2010 (Est.).* New Delhi: Automotive Tyre Manufacturers Association.

Bajaj Auto. 2007. *Bajaj Presentation: October 2007.* Pune: Bajaj Auto Ltd.

Beise, Marian. 2004. "Lead Markets: Country-Specific Success Factors of the Global Diffusion of Innovations." *Research Policy* 33: 997–1018.

Beise, Marian, and Thomas Cleff. 2004. "Assessing the Lead Market Potential of Countries for Innovation Projects." *Journal of International Management* 10: 453–477.

Bhargava, R. C. 2010. *The Maruti Story: How a Public Sector Put India on Wheels.* New Delhi: HarperCollins.

Bruche, Gert. 2010. *Tata Motor's Transformational Resource Acquisition Path—A Case Study of Latecomer Catch-up in a Business Group Context.* Berlin: Institute of Management, Berlin School of Economics and Law.

Chugan, Pawan Kumar. 1995. *Foreign Collaboration and Export Restrictions in Indian Industry: A Study of Automotive Components Industry.* Mumbai: Himalaya Publishing House.

D'Costa, Anthony P. 1995. "The Restructuring of the Indian Automobile Industry: Indian State and Japanese Capital." *World Development* 23(3): 485–502.

Doner, Richard F. 1988. "Weak State: Strong Country? The Thai Automobile Case." *Third World Quarterly* 10(4): 1542–1564.

———. 1991. *Driving a Bargain: Automobile Industrialization and Japanese Firms in Southeast Asia.* Berkeley: University of California Press.

Doz, Yves L. 1986. "Government Policies and Global Industries." In Porter, Michael E., ed. 1986. *Competition in Global Industries.* Boston, Massachusetts: Harvard Business School Press.

Doz, Yves L., and Coimbatore Krishnarao Prahalad. 1980. "How MNCs Cope with Host Government Intervention." *Harvard Business Review* 58(2): 149–157.

Economic Times. 2011. "ARAI To Have Advanced Labs for Developing Euro 5/6 Technology," *Economic Times,* August 2. Retrieved on February 14, 2011, from http://economictimes.indiatimes.com/articleshow/7453713.cms.

Ernst, Dieter. 2002. "Global Production Networks and the Changing Geography of Innovation Systems: Implications for Developing Countries." *Economics of Innovation and New Technology* 11(6): 497–523.

———. 2005. "Pathways to Innovation in Asia's Leading Electronics-exporting Countries: A Framework for Exploring Drivers and Policy Implications." *International Journal of Technology Management* 29(1/2): 6–20.

———. 2007. "Innovation Offshoring: Root Causes of Asia's Rise and Policy Implications." In Palacios, Juan J., ed. 2007. *Multinational Corporations and the Emerging Network Economy in the Pacific Rim.* New York: Routledge.

Ernst, Dieter, and Linsu Kim. 2002. "Global Production Networks, Knowledge Diffusion, and Local Capability Formation." *Research Policy* 31: 1417–1429.

Evans, Peter B. 1995. *Embedded Autonomy: States and Industrial Transformation.* Princeton, New Jersey: Princeton University Press.

Freeman, Chris. 2002. "Continental, National and Sub-national Innovation Systems—Complementarity and Economic Growth." *Research Policy* 31: 191–211.

Gilpin, Robert. 1971. "The Politics of Transnational Economic Relations." *International Organization* 25(3): 398–419.

———. 1987. *The Political Economy of International Relations.* Princeton, New Jersey: Princeton University Press.

————. 1996. "Economic Evolution of National Systems." *International Studies Quarterly* 40(3): 411–431.

Government of India (GOI). 1951. *1st Five Year Plan*. New Delhi: Planning Commission, Government of India.

————. 1956. *2nd Five Year Plan*. New Delhi: Planning Commission, Government of India.

————. 1969. *4th Five Year Plan*. New Delhi: Planning Commission, Government of India.

————. 1993. *General Budget 1993–94 General Discussion*. New Delhi: Parliament of India, Government of India.

————. 2002. *Auto Policy, March 2002*. New Delhi: Department of Heavy Industry, Ministry of Heavy Industries and Public Enterprises, Government of India.

————. 2006a. *Automotive Mission Plan 2006–2016*. New Delhi: Department of Heavy Industry, Ministry of Heavy Industries and Public Enterprises, Government of India.

————. 2006b. *Report of Working Group on Automotive Industry: Eleventh Five Year Plan (2007–2012)*. New Delhi: Department of Heavy Industry, Ministry of Heavy Industries and Public Enterprises, Government of India.

————. 2008a. *Fact Sheet on Foreign Direct Investment (FDI): From August 1991 to March 2008*. New Delhi: Department of Industrial Policy and Promotion, Ministry of Commerce and Industry, Government of India.

————. 2008b. *History*. New Delhi: Tariff Commission, Ministry of Commerce and Industry, Government of India.

————. 2008c. *India's Industrial Policies from 1948 to 1991*. New Delhi: Office of the Development Commissioner (Small Scale Industries), Ministry of Small Scale Industries, Government of India.

————. 2010. *Fact Sheet on Foreign Direct Investment (FDI): From August 1991 to November 2010*. New Delhi: Department of Industrial Policy and Promotion, Ministry of Commerce and Industry, Government of India.

Griliches, Zvi. 1957. "Hybrid Corn: An Exploration in the Economics of Technological Change." *Econometrica* 25(4): 501–522.

Hall, Robert E., and Charles I. Jones. 1999. "Why Do Some Countries Produce so Much More Output per Worker Than Others." *Quarterly Journal of Economics* 114(1): 83–116.

Herstatt, Cornelius, Rajnish Tiwari, Dieter Ernst, and Stephan Buse. 2008. *India's National Innovation System: Key Elements and Corporate Perspectives*. Working Papers, Economics Series, No. 96. Honolulu, Hawaii: East-West Center.

India Brand Equity Foundation (IBEF). 2005. *Automotive Industry on Fast Track*. New Delhi: India Brand Equity Foundation.

————. 2008. *Automotive Market and Opportunities*. New Delhi: India Brand Equity Foundation.

————. 2010. *Automotives*. New Delhi: India Brand Equity Foundation.

INTEC (Netzwerk Internationale Technologiekooperationen). 2007. *The Indian Automotive Industry*. Netzwerk Internationale Technologiekooperationen, ed. Berlin: Arbeitsgemeinschaft industrieller Forschungsvereinigungen, Otto von Guericke e.V.

Jänicke, Martin. 2005. "Trend-setters in Environmental Policy: The Character and Role of Pioneer Countries." *European Environment* 15: 129–142.

Jänicke, Martin, and Klaus Jacob. 2004. "Lead Markets for Environmental Innovations: A New Role for the Nation State." *Global Environmental Politics* 4(1): 29–46.

Jenkins, Rhys. 1977. *Dependent Industrialization in Latin America: The Automotive Industry in Argentina, Chile, and Mexico*. New York: Prager Publishers.

———. 1987. *Transnational Corporations and the Latin American Automobile Industry*. Basingstoke, Hampshire: Macmillan.

Kathuria, Sanjay. 1996. *Competing through Technology and Manufacturing: A Study of the Indian Commercial Vehicles Industry*. Delhi: Oxford University Press.

Knowledge@Wharton. 2005. *How R&D Is Changing Indian Pharma and Auto Companies*. Philadelphia, Pennsylvania: Wharton School of the University of Pennsylvania.

KPMG. 2010. *The Indian Automotive Industry: Evolving Dynamics*. Mumbai: KPMG India.

Lall, Sanjaya. 2003. *Reinventing Industrial Strategy: The Role of Government Policy in Building Industrial Competitiveness*. Oxford: International Development Centre.

Lindblom, Charles E. 1966. "Has India an Economic Future?" *Foreign Affairs* 44(2): 239–252.

Linder, Staffan Burenstam. 1961. *An Essay on Trade and Transformation*. Stockholm: Almqvist and Wiksell.

Lundvall, Bengt-Åke. 1998. "Why Study National Systems and National Styles of Innovation?" *Technology Analysis and Strategic Management* 10(4): 403–422.

Lundvall, Bengt-Åke, Björn Johnson, Esben Sloth Andersen, and Bent Dalum. 2002. "National Systems of Production, Innovation and Competence Building." *Research Policy* 31: 213–231.

Narayanan, K. 1998. "Technology Acquisition, De-regulation and Competitiveness: A Study of Indian Automobile Industry." *Research Policy* 27(2): 215–228.

———. 2004. "Technology Acquisition and Growth of Firms: Indian Automobile Sector under Changing Policy Regimes." *Economic and Political Weekly* 39(5): 461–470.

Nath, Pradosh, G.D. Sandhya, N. Mrinalini, P. R. Bose, Sujit Bhattacharya, Sandhya Wakdikar, Vipan Kumar, S.C. Sharma, Rammi Kapoor, Kashmiri Lal, and Arvind Bhardwaj. 2006. *Status of Innovation: Automotive Industry of India*. New Delhi: National Institute of Science, Technology, and Development Studies.

Nelson, Richard R., ed. 1993. *National Innovation Systems: A Comparative Analysis.* Oxford: Oxford University Press.

Niosi, Jorge. 2002. "National Systems of Innovations Are 'X-efficient' (and X-effective): Why Some Are Slow Learners." *Research Policy* 31: 291–302.

North, Douglass C. 1989. "Institutions and Economic Growth: An Historical Introduction." *World Development* 17(9): 1319–1332.

Odagiri, Hiroyuki, and Akira Goto. 1993. "The Japanese System of Innovaton: Past, Present, and Future." In Nelson, Richard R., ed. 1993. *National Innovation Systems: A Comparative Analysis.* Oxford: Oxford University Press.

Organisation for Economic Co-operation and Development (OECD). 2002. *Dynamising National Innovation Systems.* Paris: Organisation for Economic Co-operation and Development.

Organisation Internationale des Constructeurs d'Automobiles (OICA). 2000. *1999 Production Statistics.* Paris: Organisation Internationale des Constructeurs d'Automobiles (International Organization of Motor Vehicle Manufacturers).

———. 2009. *2008 Production Statistics.* Paris: Organisation Internationale des Constructeurs d'Automobiles (International Organization of Motor Vehicle Manufacturers).

———. 2010a. *2009 Production Statistics.* Paris: Organisation Internationale des Constructeurs d'Automobiles (International Organization of Motor Vehicle Manufacturers).

———. 2010b. *Economic Contributions (Updated 2007).* From http://oica.net /category/economic-contributions/auto-jobs/.

Pinglé, Vibha. 1999. *Rethinking the Developmental State: India's Industry in Comparative Perspective.* New York: Palgrave Macmillan.

Porter, Michael E. 1990. *The Competitive Advantage of Nations.* New York: Free Press.

Pradhan, Jaya Prakash, and Neelam Singh. 2009. "Outward FDI and Knowledge Flows: A Study of the Indian Automotive Sector." *International Journal of Institutions and Economies* 1(1): 106–133.

Ranawat, Mahipat, and Rajnish Tiwari. 2009. *Influence of Government Policies on Industry Development: The Case of India's Automotive Industry.* Working paper no. 57. Hamburg: Institute of Technology and Innovation Management, Hamburg University of Technology.

Rasiah, Rajah. 2007. "Export Orientation and Technological Intensities in Auto Parts Firms in East and Southeast Asia: Does Ownership Matter?" *Asian Economic Papers* 6(2): 55–76.

———. 2009. "Technological Capabilities of Automotive Firms in Indonesia and Malaysia." *Asian Economic Papers* 8(1): 151–169.

———. n.d. *Foreign Ownership, and Learning and Innovation in the Automotive Firms in Brazil, India and South Africa: The Role of Institutions in Technological Capability Building.* Programme for Technology and Management for Development, Working Paper SLPTMD-WP-024. Oxford: University of Oxford, Department of International Development.

Rasiah, Rajah, and Abdusy Syakur Amin. 2010. "Ownership and Technological Capabilities in Indonesia's Automotive Parts Firms." *Journal of the Asia Pacific Economy* 15(3): 288–300.

Rasiah, Rajah, and Ashish Kumar. 2008. "Foreign Ownership, Technological Intensities and Economic Performance of Automotive Parts Firms in India." *Asia Pacific Business Review* 14(1): 85–102.

Reserve Bank of India (RBI). 2010. *Handbook of Statistics on the Indian Economy.* Mumbai: Reserve Bank of India.

Rennings, Klaus, and Wilko Smidt. 2008. *A Lead Market Approach Towards the Emergence and Diffusion of Coal-fired Power Plant Technology.* Mannheim: ZEW (Zentrum für Europäische Wirtschaftsforschung GmbH) – Center for European Economic Research.

Rodrik, Dani. 1995. "Getting Interventions Right: How South Korea and Taiwan Grew Rich." *Economic Policy* 10(1): 55–107.

———. 2000. "Institutions for High-Quality Growth: What They Are and How to Acquire Them." *Studies in Comparative International Development* 35(3): 3–31.

Sahoo, Tapan. 2010. *Strategic Technology Management in Auto Component Industry in India.* Delhi: Indian Institute of Technology.

Society of Indian Automobile Manufacturers (SIAM). 2008a. *Economic Affairs.* New Delhi: Society of Indian Automobile Manufacturers.

———. 2008b. *Industry Statistics.* New Delhi: Society of Indian Automobile Manufacturers.

———. 2008c. *Production and Sales Flash Report for March 2008.* New Delhi: Society of Indian Automobile Manufacturers.

———. 2010a. *Economic Affairs.* New Delhi: Society of Indian Automobile Manufacturers.

———. 2010b. *Industry Statistics.* New Delhi: Society of Indian Automobile Manufacturers.

Singh, Neelam. 2004. *Strategic Approach to Strengthening the International Competitiveness in Knowledge Based Industries: The Case of Indian Automotive Industry.* New Delhi: Research and Information Systems for the Non-Aligned and Other Developing Countries (RIS).

Sumantran, V., K. Ramchand, and David J. Andrea. 1993. *The Indian Automobile Industry: A Primer Describing Its Evolution and Current State.* Ann Arbor, Michigan: Office for the Study of Automotive Transportation, University of Michigan Transportation Research Institute.

Sutton, John. 2005. "The Globalization Process: Auto-component Supply Chains in China and India." In Bourguignon, François, Boris Pleskovic, and André Sapir, eds. 2005. *Annual World Bank Conference on Development Economics Europe 2005: Are We on Track to Achieve the Millennium Development Goals?* New York: World Bank and Oxford University Press.

Technology Information, Forecasting, and Assessment Council (TIFAC). 2006. *FDI in the R&D Sector: Study for the Pattern in 1998–2003*. New Delhi: Technology Information, Forecasting, and Assessment Council.

Tiwari, Rajnish, and Cornelius Herstatt. 2010. "The Emergence of Indian Multinational Enterprises: An Empirical Study of the Motives, Current Status, and Trends of Indian Investment in Germany." In Sauvant, Karl P., Jaya Prakash Pradhan, Ayesha Chatterjee, and Brian Harley, eds. 2010. *The Rise of Indian Multinationals: Perspectives on Indian Outward Foreign Direct Investment*. New York: Palgrave Macmillan.

Tiwari, Rajnish, Mahipat Ranawat, and Andreas Lange. 2009. *India's Long March to a Global Auto Major: A Study of Government Influence on Industry Development in the Post-Independence Era*. Hamburg: Institute of Technology and Innovation Management, Hamburg University of Technology.

Torjman, Sherri. 2005. *What Is Policy?* Ottawa: Caledon Institute of Social Policy.

Vernon, Raymond. 1966. "International Investment and International Trade in the Product Cycle." *Quarterly Journal of Economics* 80(2): 190–207.

White, Lawrence J. 1971. *The Automobile Industry since 1945*. Cambridge, Massachusetts: Harvard University Press.

World Trade Organization (WTO). 2001. *International Trade Statistics 2001*. Geneva: World Trade Organization.

———. 2009. *International Trade Statistics 2009*. Geneva: World Trade Organization.

———. 2010. *International Trade Statistics 2010*. Geneva: World Trade Organization.

Yee, Amy. 2007. "Research and Development: Spending Rockets to Match Returns." *Financial Times (Special Report: India and Globalisation)*, January 26.

Policy Studies series
A publication of the East-West Center

Series Editors: Edward Aspinall and Dieter Ernst

Description
Policy Studies provides policy-relevant scholarly analysis of key contemporary domestic and international issues affecting Asia. The editors invite contributions on Asia's economics, politics, security, and international relations.

Notes to Contributors
Submissions may take the form of a proposal or complete manuscript. For more information on the Policy Studies series, please contact the Series Editors.

Editors, *Policy Studies*
East-West Center
1601 East-West Road
Honolulu, Hawai'i 96848-1601
Tel: 808.944.7197
Publications@EastWestCenter.org
EastWestCenter.org/policystudies